THORNY
ISSUES

IN CONSUMER BANKRUPTCY CASES

WRITTEN BY

JACK F. WILLIAMS AND SUSAN SEABURY

Robert M. Zinman Resident Scholar
American Bankruptcy Institute

AMERICAN
BANKRUPTCY
INSTITUTE

Copyright © 2008 by the American Bankruptcy Institute.

All rights reserved. No part of this publication may be reproduced, stored in a retrieval system or transmitted in any form or by any means electronic, mechanical, photocopying, recording or otherwise, without the prior permission of the publisher and copyright holder. Printed in the United States of America.

"This publication is designed to provide accurate and authoritative information in regard to the subject matter covered. It is sold with the understanding that the publisher is not engaged in rendering legal, accounting or other professional services. If legal advice or other expert assistance is required, the services of a competent professional person should be sought."

—From a Declaration of Principles jointly adopted by a Committee of the American Bar Association and a Committee of Publishers and Associations.

ISBN: 978-0-9818655-3-9

Additional copies may be purchased from the American Bankruptcy Institute. Discounts are available to ABI members. Copies also may be purchased at ABI's Web site, ABI World, www.abiworld.org.

Founded on Capitol Hill in 1982, the American Bankruptcy Institute (ABI) is the only multi-disciplinary, nonpartisan organization devoted to the advancement of jurisprudence related to problems of insolvency. The ABI membership includes more than 11,500 attorneys, bankers, judges, accountants, professors, turnaround specialists and other bankruptcy professionals, providing a forum for the exchange of ideas and information. ABI was founded to provide Congress with unbiased testimony and research on insolvency issues.

For further information, contact:

American Bankruptcy Institute

44 Canal Center Plaza, Suite 400, Alexandria, VA 22314

(703) 739-0800 • (703) 739-1060 Fax

www.abiworld.org

Acknowledgments

ABI and the authors acknowledge and appreciate the efforts of the speakers from the two American Bankruptcy Institute (ABI) webinars based upon these materials. They assisted in refining the subject matter, identifying relevant cases and reviewing the materials. The speakers were: Hon. Marvin A. Isgur, U.S. Bankruptcy Court (S.D. Tex.), Houston; David G. Peake, chapter 13 trustee, Houston; Janet Northrup, attorney and chapter 7 trustee, Houston; Ramona D. Elliott, General Counsel, Executive Office for U.S. Trustees; Hon. Howard R. Tallman, U.S. Bankruptcy Court (D. Colo), Denver; Sally Zeman, chapter 13 trustee, Denver; and Ellen R. Welner, attorney, George T. Carlson & Associates, Englewood, Colo. ABI and the authors would also like to extend their gratitude to Judge Isgur for his assistance in outlining the topics that would be of interest to consumer bankruptcy professionals. Finally, ABI and the authors would like to give a special thanks to Prof. Williams' research assistant George Bara and West Publishing for their help in gathering cases to be included in the appendix. The layout and production of this book were handled by ABI staff: Carolyn Kanon, Communications Director, and Traci Van Buren, Communications Assistant.

Sponsors

The American Bankruptcy Institute is grateful to the following firms, associations and individuals who provided financial support for the publishing of this handbook:

BECKET&LEE LLP
ATTORNEYS AT LAW

BRICE, VANDER
LINDEN & WERNICK, P.C.

REBECCA CONNELLY

GOLD LANGE AND MAJOROS, P.C.

Kilpatrick
Associates

About the Authors

Professor Jack F. Williams, JD, CIRA, CDBV

Jack F. Williams is a professor at Georgia State University College of Law and the Middle East Institute in Atlanta, where he teaches and/or conducts research in the areas of bankruptcy and business reorganizations, mergers and acquisitions, corporate finance, taxation, Islamic Commercial Law and law and terrorism. Prof. Williams served as ABI's inaugural Robert M. Zinman ABI Scholar in Residence (2001) and has returned to that post a second time for 2008. He is also the Association of Insolvency and Restructuring Advisors' Scholar in Residence (2004-present). He is a managing director at BDO Consulting in the New York and Atlanta offices, where his areas of focus include restructuring and financial advisory services, financial fraud and fraudulent transfers, distressed business valuations, restructuring and insolvency taxation, forensic accounting, commercial damages modeling, investigation, litigation consulting and the foreign corrupt practices act. Prof. Williams has served as an arbitrator and as a mediator, and as an expert witness/consultant in solvency, intercompany, fraudulent transfer, preference, tax, valuation, commercial damages, excessive force in conflict and counter-terrorism engagements. He has also served as the tax adviser to the National Bankruptcy Review Commission and as its Tax Advisory Committee chair. Prof. Williams has also served as chair of ABI's Bankruptcy Taxation Committee, as reporter (taxation) for the ABI Bankruptcy Code Review Project, as dean of the American Board of Certification, as a commentator on the Republic of Croatia's and Bulgaria's Bankruptcy Codes and as a co-drafter of the Russian Federation's Energy and Natural Resources Taxation Code. He has taught bankruptcy taxation to attorneys in the Office of Chief Counsel, IRS, as part of the New York University School of Law/IRS Continuing Professional Education Program to attorneys in the U.S. Department of Justice, to attorneys and other professionals in the Office of the U.S. Trustee and to bankruptcy judges as part of the U.S. Federal Judicial Center educational programming. Prof. Williams is a Fellow in the American College of Bankruptcy, has written seven books and more than 150 articles, and speaks frequently on a number of topics at various functions.

Susan H. Seabury, MBA, JD

Susan H. Seabury is a director and special counsel with BDO Consulting, a division of BDO Seidman LLP in Atlanta. She has represented debtors, creditors and creditors' committees both as counsel and as a financial advisor. Ms. Seabury has developed a model for preference litigation that has been used in several cases in multiple jurisdictions. She has also prepared expert reports for litigation in the areas of fraudulent conveyances and plan feasibility. Her case involvements have included a variety of industries including retail, real estate, transportation, hedge funds, telecommunications and wholesale distributions. Previously, Ms. Seabury practiced law with Lamberth, Bonapfel, Cifelli & Stokes, PA and with Kilpatrick Stockton LLP. She is a member of the Georgia Bar, several Federal Bars, the Atlanta Bar, ABI, the Association of Insolvency and Restructuring Advisors and the International Women in Restructuring Confederation. She has authored or co-authored several articles, including "Bankruptcy and Debt under the Servicemember Civil Relief Act," forthcoming in the *2008 Norton Annual Review* (with Jack F. Williams); "Squaring Bankruptcy Valuation Practice with *Daubert* Demands," 16 Am. Bankr. Inst. L. Rev. 161 (Spring 2008) (with Hon. Stan Bernstein and Jack F. Williams); and "The Role of Financial Testimony in Bankruptcy after *Daubert*," 80 Am. Bankr. L.J. 101 (2007) (with Hon. Stan Bernstein and Jack F. Williams). Ms. Seabury is also a contributing author to *Norton Bankruptcy Law and Practice* (3rd ed.). She has a B.A. in economics from Vanderbilt University, an M.B.A from the Owen Graduate School of Management at Vanderbilt University and a J.D. *cum laude* from Georgia State University College of Law.

About the Editor

 *Felicia S. Turner,* JD

Felicia S. Turner became the Deputy Executive Director of the American Bankruptcy Institute in September 2007. Immediately prior, she was the U.S. Trustee for Regions 20 and 21, managing 12 offices covering 13 federal judicial districts and four federal circuits in Georgia, Florida, Puerto Rico, the U.S. Virgin Islands, Oklahoma, Kansas and New Mexico. She oversaw the coordination of the U.S. Trustee offices' participation in bankruptcy cases under all chapters to preserve the integrity of the judicial system, including the development and implementation of policy and ensuring regional and national consistency in and appropriateness of the federal government's legal positions. Prior to her appointment in 2003 as the U.S. Trustee for Region 21, Ms. Turner was a partner in the Atlanta-based law firm of Troutman Sanders, LLP, where she was a member of its bankruptcy practice group and litigation section, mainly representing creditors and debtors in chapter 11 cases. Before joining Troutman Sanders in 1999, she practiced with Sullivan, Mountjoy, Stainback & Miller, PSC, in Owensboro, Ky., where her work ranged from representing debtors and creditors in consumer cases to serving as debtor-in-possession counsel for Big Rivers Electric Corporation. Ms. Turner is a frequent panelist and speaker at ABI and bar meetings all over the country and previously served on ABI's Caribbean Insolvency Symposium Advisory Board. During 2005, she served on the U.S. Trustee Program's committee for implementation of the provisions of the Bankruptcy

Abuse Prevention and Consumer Protection Act of 2005. Until taking her current position, she also served on the National Conference of Bankruptcy Judges' liaison committee with the U.S. Trustee Program. Ms. Turner received her law degree from Duke University School of Law in Durham, N.C. in 1994 and her undergraduate degree in mathematics *magna cum laude* from DePauw University in Greencastle, Ind., in 1991.

Table of Contents

Editor's Notes

During 2007-08, the American Bankruptcy Institute conducted four successful webinars in its "Consumer Bankruptcy in Practice" series. The first and second in the series were based in Atlanta and Tennessee, respectively, and addressed means testing and projected disposable income issues. The third and fourth in the series were based in Houston and Denver, respectively, and addressed some "hot and not-so-easy" issues in consumer cases, such as getting the discharge, paying debtor and creditor counsel in chapter 13, credit counseling and debtor education, and post-confirmation modifications. In this book, we have compiled the materials from the third and fourth sessions. In designing the webinar program and the related materials, it was not ABI's intention to cover the well-worn path of a general introduction to the practice of consumer bankruptcy. Rather, our intent was to focus on a few recurring thorny issues where there are few clearly defined answers. To assist with the understanding, and hopefully the resolution, of these issues, both sides of the argument are presented. Further, in some areas, decisions that were subsequently overturned are presented to help the practitioner understand the developments of the current positions on a given issue. Although these materials have many citations to cases from the Fifth and Tenth Circuits due to the "location" of the webinars, they contain citations from all over the country as well and an excellent discussion of the issues. To purchase the audio recordings from any of the webinars in this series, please visit the Distance Learning section of ABI's consumer Web site at consumer.abiworld.org.

I.

Consumer Discharge

A. Introduction

Most individual debtors entering modern bankruptcy seek one resolution – a discharge of their indebtedness.[1] Along with exemptions and the carve-out of future income from property of the estate under §541(a)(6)[2] for chapter 7 cases, the discharge fuels the fresh start of the debtor, a policy of singular importance in individual bankruptcies. Individual debtors can also obtain a discharge under chapters 11 and 13 of the Bankruptcy Code, although the chapter 11 discharge for an individual conforms more to the new chapter 13 discharge regarding timing.[3] The discharge represents the heart of the fresh-start policy promoted by the Code. A court generally grants the discharge as a matter of course unless an objecting party can establish that the debtor has engaged in certain prohibited conduct, usually some type of fraud or bankruptcy crime.[4] The objecting party has the burden of establishing a ground for the denial of a discharge.

If a debtor has been denied a discharge in a bankruptcy case, so that all his debts remain outstanding, the debtor may not include the same

---

1   *See* 11 U.S.C. §727.
2   All section and chapter references in these materials, unless otherwise noted, refer to title 11 of the U.S. Code, also known as the "Bankruptcy Code."
3   *See* 11 U.S.C. §§1141(d) and 1328(a) and (b).
4   *See* 11 U.S.C. §727(a).

obligations in a subsequent case to obtain a chapter 7 discharge. The denial of the discharge is *res judicata* as to the obligations existing at that time, which are forever nondischargeable.

A discharge in a bankruptcy case terminates any personal liability on the part of the debtor with regard to a pre-petition debt and operates as an injunction against the commencement or continuation of an action, the employment of process, or any act, including telephone calls, letters and personal contacts to collect, recover or offset any discharged debt.[5] In effect, the discharge is a total prohibition on debt collection efforts against the debtor. Further, under §524, any attempt to reaffirm a particular debt is void unless the particular provisions of the Bankruptcy Code delineating the requirements of reaffirmation are specifically followed.[6] Note, however, that the discharge does not void a judgment or debt in its entirety; rather it only discharges the debtor's obligation to pay. Therefore, the discharge generally does not impact the obligations and liabilities of any co-obligors.

B. Chapter 7 Discharge

The scope of the chapter 7 discharge is quite broad. Any debt that arose prior to the entry of the order for relief is discharged.[7] Under §727(a), the bankruptcy court must grant the individual debtor a discharge of all debts that arose before the order for relief unless one of the 12 conditions is met.[8]

Section 727(d) requires the court to revoke a discharge already granted in certain circumstances. There is a revocation if the debtor obtains a discharge through fraud, acquired and concealed property of the estate, or refused to obey a court order to testify. Additionally, §727(e) permits the trustee, a creditor or the U.S. Trustee[9] to request revocation of a discharge within one year after the discharge is granted for fraud.

---

5   *Id.*

6   *See generally* 11 U.S.C. §524(c).

7   *See* 11 U.S.C. §727(b).

8   *See* 11 U.S.C. §727(a).

9   When using the term "U.S. Trustee" herein, the reader should construe same to include the Bankruptcy Administrators in North Carolina and Alabama.

A debtor may waive his right to discharge under §727(a)(10) of the Bankruptcy Code. The waiver of discharge must be executed in writing by the debtor after the order for relief under chapter 7 has been entered. The waiver is ineffective until approved by the court.

C. Chapter 13 Discharge

The court grants the chapter 13 discharge not at plan confirmation, but rather after the debtor has completed performance under the chapter 13 plan. Although significantly curtailed by the Bankruptcy Abuse Prevention and Consumer Protection Act of 2005 (BAPCPA), under §1328(a), many of the debtor's obligations are discharged, even some generally deemed nondischargeable under §523(a). Notwithstanding the limits put in place by BAPCPA, the chapter 13 discharge still appears to be broadest in scope, discharging all debts provided for in the plan or disallowed under §502. In fact, only (a) domestic support obligations, (b) certain §523(a) debts (but not all of such debts), (c) trust fund taxes, (d) criminal fines and restitution, (e) civil restitution or damages awarded for certain types of willful or malicious injury,[10] and (f) certain long-term debts that the plan purports to pay out after the plan survive the chapter 13 discharge.

Filing under chapter 13 provides other benefits, including: (a) the curing of mortgage arrearages and prevention of foreclosure; (b) the payment of priority/nondischargeable tax obligations through the plan without incurring post-petition interest; (c) capping the payment to secured creditors on their secured claims at the plan confirmation value, allowing the debtor to benefit from post-confirmation appreciation; and (d) the retention by the debtor of certain tax attributes generally lost in a chapter 7 or 11 filing.

A chapter 13 debtor failing to complete payments under the chapter 13 plan for reasons beyond the debtor's control may nevertheless be granted a "hardship" discharge under §1328(b). This hardship discharge is granted so long as: (1) the creditors have received as much under the plan as they would have under a chapter 7 liquidation; (2) the debtor's failure to complete payments is due to circumstances

---

10   *Compare with* 11 U.S.C. §523(a)(6) ("willful *and* malicious...") (emphasis added).

for which the debtor should not justly be held accountable; and (3) modification of the plan is not practicable. In effect, the hardship discharge is a chapter 7 discharge granted in a chapter 13 case. Thus, all debts nondischargeable under §523(a) that could have been discharged pursuant to completion of the chapter 13 plan remain in full force and effect, as in a chapter 7 case.

D. Debtors Ineligible for a Discharge

As noted above, some potential debtors are ineligible for a discharge for a variety of reasons delineated in §727(a). This section of the materials considers the difficult issue of timing under §§727(a) and 1328(f) and the special matter of the subsequent bankruptcy filing and previous discharge.

1. Time Limit from Chapter 7 to Chapter 7

BAPCPA amended §727(a)(8) such that a debtor may not obtain a chapter 7 discharge if he/she had been granted a chapter 7 discharge "in a case commenced within 8 years before the date of the filing of the petition." The only modification here was a change from the pre-BAPCPA six years to the present eight years.[11] This leaves the pre-BAPCPA question of how this period should be calculated.

There are no Southern District of Texas or Fifth Circuit cases construing §727(a)(8) post-BAPCPA. However, other than a change to the length of time as noted above, the language of §727(a)(8) is the same in the pre- and post-BAPCPA versions. In a pre-BAPCPA case, the Southern District of Texas bankruptcy court held that the time period runs from the date the first chapter 7 petition was filed to the date the second chapter 7 was filed.[12] In *In re Cauthen*, 152 B.R. 149 (Bankr. S.D. Tex. 1993), the bankruptcy court held that a debtor could not be granted a discharge when the current case was filed within six years of the filing of the prior case in which the debtor had received a chapter 7 discharge. It also appears that the court found that the debtor was an abusive filer. In response to a pattern or practice of bankruptcy abuse by a debtor, the court held that an appropriate sanction included the issuance of an

---

11   11 U.S.C. §727(a)(8).
12   *In re Cauthen*, 152 B.R. 149, 153 (Bankr. S.D. Tex. 1993).

injunction to prevent the debtor's filing of any bankruptcy petitions in violation of the law.

The general consensus outside of the Fifth Circuit appears to be the same; that is, the time period begins when the first chapter 7 was filed and ends when the second chapter 7 case was filed. For example, in *In re Mayo,* 2007 WL 1074078 (Bankr. D. Md. Jan. 12, 2007), the court found that the debtor had commenced the prior case on Nov. 13, 2000. The court noted that in that prior case, the debtor had received a chapter 7 discharge on Feb. 21, 2001. The court then compared the petition date of the subsequent case, Dec. 27, 2005, to the petition date of the prior case and found that less than eight years had passed. Note that the court held that even if the first case commenced pre-BAPCPA, the eight-year period (and not the six-year period) still applied to the current case. *In re McKittrick,* 349 B.R. 569 (Bankr. W.D. Wis. 2006), is in accordance with this particular aspect of the holding. In that case, the court held that modifying the future eligibility of a debtor to receive a discharge in bankruptcy is, in general, simply part of Congress' power under the bankruptcy clause of the Constitution. Thus, the change from six to eight years between discharges affected the debtor to her detriment where the statute was amended between her two cases.

Moreover, it appears that the U.S. Trustee may bring an adversary proceeding to determine eligibility for discharge on this point even though no creditor has objected.[13]

2. Time Limit from Chapter 7 to Chapter 13

BAPCPA amended §1328(f)(1) such that "a court shall not grant a discharge . . . if a debtor has received a discharge—(1) in a case filed under chapter 7, 11 or 12 . . . during the 4-year period preceding the date of the order for relief under this chapter."

There are no cases from the Southern District of Texas or the Fifth Circuit construing §1328(f)(1). Elsewhere, the consensus is that the look-back period runs from filing date to filing date, a result consistent with the approach embraced by the cases construing §727(a)(8) as noted above, notwithstanding the differences in the relevant texts. However,

---

13   *See In re McKittrick,* 349 B.R. 569 (Bankr. W.D. Wis. 2006).

one bankruptcy court ruled that the period was from discharge date to filing date but was recently reversed by the district court.[14]

Presently, the only reported court of appeals case on this point is *In re Bateman,* 515 F.3d 272 (4th Cir. 2008). In that case, the Fourth Circuit denied a discharge to a chapter 13 debtor who previously received a discharge in another chapter 13 case. The court interpreted §1328(f) (2) (which has the same "filed under" language as (f)(1)) as barring the debtor from obtaining a discharge in the current chapter 13 case, not if the debtor received a prior chapter 13 discharge pursuant to a discharge order entered less than two years before order for relief in the current case, but only if the debtor received a discharge in a prior case that was filed less than two years before order for relief in the current case.

In *Sanders v. Carroll,* 2008 WL 275678 (E.D. Mich. Jan. 31, 2008), the district court addressed the issues presented by §1328(f)(1), reversing the bankruptcy court on the appropriate application of §1328(f). In this case, the court held that the overwhelming majority of bankruptcy courts addressing the issue has held that, to give effect to the plain meaning of the statutory language, the look-back periods referred to in §1328(f) begin with the filing of the debtor's first bankruptcy case as opposed to the issuance of a discharge in that first case. After acknowledging what it considered to be the emerging consensus, the court adopted the reasoning and result of the overwhelming majority of bankruptcy courts, reversing the bankruptcy court. The court held that the four-year period in §1328(f)(1) begins to run on the date the debtor filed his previous chapter 7 bankruptcy case and ends on the date he filed his pending chapter 13 case.

Furthermore, in *In re Knighton,* 355 B.R. 922 (Bankr. M.D. Ga. 2006), the court stated that under the statute barring discharge in debtor's pending chapter 13 case, if a debtor received a prior discharge in a case filed under chapter 7 during the four-year period preceding the date of the order for relief in the pending case, the look-back period ran from the filing date of the prior case to the filing date of the pending case. Thus, the chapter 13 debtor was eligible for a discharge upon the completion of her pending case, given that more than four years

---

14   *See Sanders v. Carroll,* 2008 WL 275678 (E.D. Mich. Jan. 31, 2008).

I. Consumer Discharge

had passed between the filing of the debtor's prior case to the filing of pending case.

Another area of litigation centers on whether "filed under" in §1328(f) means the original case or the converted case from which the debtor received his discharge. Some debtors who filed under chapter 13, but had their cases converted to a chapter 7 and received a discharge, have argued that their cases should be considered "filed under" the earlier chapter 13 case, notwithstanding the conversion to a chapter 7 case. Those debtors assert their look-back period is the two-year period of §1328(f)(2) (time between two consecutive chapter 13 filings), rather than the four-year period of §1328(f)(1).[15] The consensus has been that the converted case is the case in which the debtor "filed under" for purposes of interpreting §1328(f), and the start of the look-back period is the date of the original case rather than the conversion date.[16] In support of this position, courts have pointed to §348, which states that conversion to another chapter constitutes relief under that converted chapter and does not change the petition date or the commencement of the case.[17]

In an extended discussion of the range of issues presented by §1328(f), the court in *In re Grydzuk,* 353 B.R. 564 (Bankr. N.D. Ind. 2006), held that §1328(f) implemented congressional intent that sought to render ineligible for discharge under chapter 13 any debtor who, within four years of entry of order for relief in the chapter 13 case, had received a discharge in "a case filed under chapter 7, 11, or 12 of this title." In effect, according to the court, Congress sought to preclude the filing of a "20" (chapter 7 followed by chapter 13), a "24" (chapter 11 followed by chapter 13), and a "25" (chapter 12 followed by chapter 13), for a more extended period of time than a "26" (back-to-back chapter 13 cases). Thus, the discharge referred to in §1328(f)(1) refers to the chapter under which the discharge was actually entered, rather than the chapter under which the earlier case was initiated. Here the debtor converted the previous case from chapter 13 to 7.

---

15   *E.g., In re Grice,* 373 B.R. 886 (Bankr. E.D. Wis. 2007); *In re Ybarra,* 359 B.R. 702 (Bankr. S.D. Ill. 2007); *In re Knighton,* 355 B.R. 922 (Bankr. M.D. Ga. 2006); *In re Grydzuk,* 353 B.R. 564 (Bankr. N.D. Ind. 2006); *In re Capers,* 347 B.R. 169 (Bankr. D. S.C. 2006).

16   *In re Sours,* 350 B.R. 261 (Bankr. E.D. Va. 2006).

17   *Id.* at 267-8.

In *In re Capers,* 347 B.R. 169 (Bankr. D. S.C. 2006), the court held that §1328(f) served to prevent a chapter 13 debtor from obtaining a discharge under that chapter based on the fact that less than four years prior to the order for relief, she had received a chapter 7 discharge, notwithstanding that she had received this prior chapter 7 discharge in a case that was originally filed under chapter 13 and only later converted to one under chapter 7. The court noted that even assuming that the language of §1328(f), interpreted literally, did not operate to disqualify the debtor from obtaining a discharge under chapter 13, because the case in which she obtained a prior bankruptcy discharge was originally "filed" under chapter 13, the court had to reject such a "literal" application as clearly at odds with expressed congressional intent.

A number of cases have addressed the peculiar timing issues presented when an initial case is later converted to a different case under the Bankruptcy Code. For example, in *In re Grice,* 373 B.R. 886 (Bankr. E.D. Wis. 2007), the court observed that the bankruptcy case that the chapter 13 debtor had previously filed had to be treated as having been filed under chapter 7, the chapter to which it was converted, and not under chapter 13, the chapter under which it was originally commenced, for purposes of deciding whether the debtor was entitled to a discharge. Moreover, in *In re Sours,* 350 B.R. 261 (Bankr. E.D. Va. 2006), the court held:

> [I]t is clear to this Court that a converted case relates back to the initial filing date for all purposes, including matters relating to discharge. Section 348(a) provides that "conversion from a case under one chapter of this title to a case under another chapter of this title constitutes an order for relief under the chapter to which the case is converted." 11 U.S.C. §348(a). Thus, the Court agrees with the United States Trustee that §348(a) mandates that a case which has been converted to Chapter 7 from Chapter 13, such as the Debtors' Prior Case, is deemed to be "filed under" Chapter 7 on the date on which the Chapter 13 was filed. Accordingly, this Court also finds that Section 348(a) mandates that it is the original filing date of a case, not the conversion date, which controls the running of the time-bar for discharge purposes. Therefore, the Debtors are subject to the four-year time restriction of §1328(f)(1) and are not eligible to receive a discharge in the Pending Case.

I. Consumer Discharge

Additionally, in *In re Ybarra*, 359 B.R. 702 (Bankr. S.D. Ill. 2007), the court held that the phrase "in a case filed" was not limited in its application only to the chapter under which the petition was initially filed in the prior case, but also included the chapter under which the petition was deemed filed if the prior case was converted from one chapter to another prior to the entry of the discharge order. Thus, the four-year "look-back" period applied to the debtors who, prior to commencement of their current chapter 13 case, had previously received a discharge in chapter 7, although this chapter 7 discharge was entered in the case that the debtors had commenced by filing their petition under chapter 13, and that was deemed to be filed under chapter 7 only when case was converted.[18]

3. Time Limit from Chapter 13 to Chapter 7

BAPCPA did not amend §727(a)(9). It provides that a debtor may not obtain a chapter 7 discharge in a case commenced within six years of the filing of a previous chapter 13 in which he obtained a discharge unless two exceptions apply. The first exception is if "payments under the plan . . . totaled at least (A) 100 percent of the allowed unsecured claims." The second exception is if those payments totaled at least "70 percent of such claims" and the plan was proposed in good faith and represents "debtor's best efforts."[19]

Presently, there are no cases from the Southern District of Texas or the Fifth Circuit construing §727(a)(9). However, the Southern District of Texas has interpreted "payments under the plan" to mean all payments made by the debtor pursuant to a chapter 13 plan.[20] Therefore,

---

18   See also *In re Khan*, 2006 WL 3716036 (Bankr. D. Md. Dec. 14, 2006) ("The absence of a like prohibition on serial filings of Chapter 7 and Chapter 13 petitions, combined with the evident care with which Congress fashioned these express prohibitions, convinces us that Congress did not intend categorically to foreclose the benefit of Chapter 13 reorganization to a debtor who previously has filed for Chapter 7 relief."); *In re Lewis*, 339 B.R. 814 (Bankr. S.D. Ga. 2006) (court held that although chapter 13 debtors' inability, based upon their history of bankruptcy filings, to obtain discharge in their current bankruptcy cases was one factor that court could consider in assessing their good faith, for plan confirmation purposes, it was not determinative of "good faith" issue, and debtors' inability to obtain discharge in chapter 13 did not require dismissal of their bankruptcy cases, on theory that they could not propose confirmable plan).

19   11 U.S.C. §727(a)(9).

20   *In re Perez*, 339 B.R. 385, 390 n.4 (Bankr. S.D. Tex. 2006) (clarifying that even if debtor pays creditor directly and that practice is commonly referred to as paying outside of plan, those payments are still "payments under the plan" pursuant to the provisions of chapter 13 plan).

even though the Southern District of Texas does not have a case yet that construes §727(a)(9), it is likely that the court would interpret §727(a)(9) to mean that payments under the plan means payments to everyone – for example the trustee, debtor's attorney, secured creditors and unsecured creditors – and not just payments to the unsecured creditors.[21]

Elsewhere, cases on this section have focused on whether payments made to unsecured creditors must total at least 100 percent or 70 percent, or if payments made to the trustee (for distribution to everyone – both unsecured creditors and others) must total at least 100 percent or 70 percent. Courts have interpreted this section using the plain-meaning approach, holding that the key is that those payments just be paid into the plan; those payments do not all have to go to unsecured creditors.[22]

In *In re Griffin,* 352 B.R. 475 (B.A.P. 8th Cir. 2006), the court held that a debtor who filed a chapter 7 case within six years of the petition date of an earlier chapter 13 case will not be denied a chapter 7 discharge if the debtor, in that chapter 13 case, paid to the trustee for distribution under debtor's plan an amount equal to 70 percent of the allowed unsecured claims and the court found that the plan was proposed by the debtor in good faith and was the debtor's best effort, or if the debtor paid to the trustee for distribution under the plan an amount that totaled at least 100 percent of the allowed unsecured claims. The *Griffin* court discussed that no case, within the context of a chapter 13 plan confirmation or discharge, has interpreted "payments under the plan" to mean payments to unsecured creditors only.[23] That court reasoned that the statute provides that a debtor may not receive a chapter 7 discharge if he received a chapter 13 discharge in a case filed within six years of the filing of the chapter 7 case "unless payments under the plan in such case totaled *at least* . . . 100 percent of the allowed unsecured claims in such case . . . (emphasis added)"[24] Since no one can pay more than 100 percent of the allowed unsecured claims to their unsecured creditors, clearly the use of "at least 100 percent"

---

21   *See In re Griffin,* 352 B.R. 475, 478 (B.A.P. 8th Cir. 2006).

22   *E.g., Griffin,* 352 B.R. at 479.

23   *Id.* at 478.

24   *Id.*

means a value equivalent that needs to be paid into the plan and not just specifically to unsecured creditors.[25]

In *In re Perez,* 339 B.R. 385 (Bankr. S.D. Tex. 2006), the court addressed a number of related issues, the first of which is relevant to this discussion. There, the court held that adequate protection payments to real estate lienholders were not "payments made under a proposed plan." The court supported this holding based on the observation that the chapter 13 trustee is statutorily required to hold such payments until the plan is confirmed.

4. Time Limit From Chapter 13 to Chapter 13

Section 1328(f)(2) states that the court shall not grant a chapter 13 discharge "if the debtor has received a discharge" in a case filed under chapter 13 "during the 2-year period preceding the date of such order."

There are no cases from the Southern District of Texas or the Fifth Circuit construing §1328(f)(2). Commentators have noted that this section generates some confusion because the two-year provision appears improbable and impractical.[26] Specifically, debtors who seek relief under chapter 13 are unlikely to have proposed a plan that is less than two years old and still obtain a discharge.[27] As such, in at least one case, the trustee proposed that the look-back period in §1328(f)(2) should be measured from the date of the prior discharge to the petition date of the current chapter 13. The court disagreed.[28] Acknowledging that chapter 13 debtors rarely complete a plan and receive a discharge within two years, the court still held that the look-back period is measured from the filing date of the first petition to the filing date of the second. Another court observed that the plain language of the statute dictated a "filing date to filing date" interpretation.[29] Moreover, the court stated that such a reading gave "effect to the logical sequence

---

25   *Id. See also Tidewater Finance Co. v. Williams,* 498 F.3d 249 (4th Cir. 2007) ("[T]he six-year waiting period in §727(a)(8) is [not] a limitations period that the bankruptcy court should have equitably tolled during [debtor's] chapter 13 proceedings.").

26   *E.g.,* William Houston Brown, *Taking Exception to a Debtor's Discharge: The 2005 Bankruptcy Amendments Make it Easier,* 79 Am. Bankr. L.J. 419, 449 (2005).

27   *Id.*

28   *In re West,* 352 B.R. 482 (Bankr. E.D. Ark. 2006).

29   *In re Graves,* 2007 WL 1075108 (Bankr. D. Md. Jan. 19, 2007).

of the language used" in §1328(f)(2).[30] The court in *In re Ward,* 370 B.R. 812 (Bankr. D. Neb. 2007), reached a similar conclusion, holding that the discharge prohibition period of §1328(f) commenced upon the filing of the first chapter 13 case.

Additionally, in *In re West,* 352 B.R. 482 (Bankr. E.D. Ark. 2006), the court held that a debtor is not entitled to a chapter 13 discharge under §1328(f)(2) if the debtor has received a discharge in a case filed under chapter 13 within two years of the current case's filing. Therefore, a debtor who received a discharge in a chapter 13 case filed more than two years before the current case is entitled to a discharge. The court determined that the two-year period was measured from the filing dates of the two cases, and not from the discharge of the first and the filing of the second.

In *In re Graves,* 2007 WL 1075108 (Bankr. D. Md. Jan. 19, 2007), the court provided an important lesson in statutory construction. In that case, the court held that the language of §1328, when applying the plain-meaning rule of statutory construction, results in the adoption of the "filing date to filing date" interpretation of §1328(f)(2). According to the court, the "filing date to filing date" approach implements §1328 the way it is written. Section 1328(f)(2) prohibits a debtor from receiving a discharge "if the debtor has received a discharge...in a case filed under chapter 13...during the 2-year period" preceding the date of the order for relief of the current case. Moreover, the court observed that the "filing date to filing date" interpretation gave effect to the logical sequence of the language used. Thus, each subsequent clause modifies the immediately preceding clause. Finally, all words are given effect and no punctuation needs to be added or deleted.

Courts construing §1328(f)(2), like courts construing §1328(f)(1), state that this subsection is a limitation rather than a disqualifier for chapter 13 relief.[31] Even though the debtor is not eligible for a discharge, the plan is still otherwise confirmable if other requirements are met.[32] To date, there are no reported cases that hold that the look-back period

---

30   *Id.* at 3. *See also In re Ward,* 370 B.R. 812 (Bankr. D. Neb. 2007).
31   *See In re Bateman,* 341 B.R. 540 (Bankr. D. Md. 2006); *In re Lewis,* 339 B.R. 814 (Bankr. S.D. Ga. 2006).
32   *Id.*

for §1328(f)(2) runs from discharge date of the previous chapter 13 case to the filing date of the new chapter 13 case. For example, in *In re Bateman,* 515 F.3d 272 (4th Cir. 2008), the court held that §1328(f)(2) had to be interpreted as barring the debtor from obtaining a discharge in the current chapter 13 case, not if the debtor received a prior chapter 13 discharge less than two years before the order for relief in the current case, but only if the debtor received a discharge in the prior case that was filed less than two years before the order for relief in the current case. However, the court tempered its ruling by holding that the debtor's inability to obtain a discharge did not make him ineligible to file for chapter 13 relief or affect the fact that the petition or the plan was filed in good faith. Similarly, the court in *In re Lewis,* 339 B.R. 814 (Bankr. S.D. Ga. 2006), held that §1328(f) was not an eligibility provision. Thus, the mere fact that the debtors were barred from obtaining discharges in their current chapter 13 cases did not, in itself, affect debtors' eligibility for chapter 13 relief.

5. More Cases

Many of the cases litigated with regard to eligibility for discharge center on whether a chapter 13 case may be filed even if a prior chapter 7 discharge was granted in an earlier case filed within four years of the current case. The consensus ruling appears to be yes. Courts have held that this section is a "limitation" rather than a "prohibition" to filing.[33] The debtor is still able to file a chapter 13 petition and may avail himself of most protections, including proposing and confirming a repayment plan, but is ineligible for a discharge in the case.[34] For example, in *In re Bateman,* 515 F.3d 272 (4th Cir. 2008), the Fourth Circuit held that a debtor is not precluded from filing in good faith a new chapter 13 bankruptcy case, even though he may be ineligible for a discharge under §1328(f). In *In re Godwin,* 2007 WL 4191729 (Bankr. M.D.N.C. Nov. 21, 2007), the court agreed that a chapter 7 discharge was not a *per se* bar to a debtor's ability to proceed under chapter 13. Finally, in *In re Sanders,* 368 B.R. 634 (Bankr. E.D. Mich. 2007), the court acknowledged that the debtor who filed his chapter

---

33   *In re Bateman,* 515 F.3d 272 (4th Cir. 2008); *In re Khan,* 2006 WL 3716036 (Bankr. D. Md. Dec. 14, 2006).

34   *In re Lewis,* 339 B.R. 814 (Bankr. S.D. Ga. 2006)

13 case within four years of his previous chapter 7 case was statutorily barred from receiving a chapter 13 discharge. However, this did not preclude confirmation of the debtor's proposed plan, if it was otherwise confirmable.

E. BAPCPA Requirements for Chapter 13 Discharges

If the debtor is otherwise eligible for a chapter 13 discharge, there are three additional components imposed by BAPCPA that the debtor must satisfy to receive a chapter 13 discharge. In summary: (1) the debtor must make a certification to the court that domestic support obligations have been satisfied; (2) he must complete a personal financial management course; and (3) after notice and a hearing, the court must enter an order finding no reasonable cause to believe that §522(q) is implicated.[35]

The first BAPCPA requirement is that "as soon as practicable" after the debtor has made all payments under the plan and for a debtor who is required by "a judicial or administrative order, or by statute, to pay a domestic support obligation," the debtor is to certify that his domestic-support obligations "due on or before the date of the certification" have been paid.[36] "Due on or before" the date of the certification includes domestic-support obligations due before the case was filed, "but only to the extent provided for by the plan...."[37]

Section 101(14A) defines "domestic support obligation" as a debt that accrues "before, on, or after" the petition date. It includes interest that accrues under applicable nonbankruptcy law. The term includes debts owed to a —

1. spouse,
2. former spouse,
3. child of debtor,
4. child's parent,
5. legal guardian,
6. responsible relative, or
7. governmental unit.[38]

---

35   11 U.S.C. §1328(a), (g) and (h).
36   11 U.S.C. §1328(a).
37   11 U.S.C. §1328(a).
38   11 U.S.C. §101(14A)(A)(i) and (ii).

Those debts must be "in the nature of"—

1. alimony,
2. maintenance,
3. or support (including assistance provided by a governmental unit).[39]

Even if a debt is not expressly designated in the above terms, so long as it is "in the nature" of the above, it will be deemed a domestic support obligation pursuant to §104(14A)(B), an approach consistent with prior law. The debt may be "established or subject to establishment before, on, or after" the petition date by separation, divorce or property settlement agreement, court order or determination made by a governmental unit, and that is "not assigned to a nongovernmental entity."[40] Even if it is voluntarily assigned to a nongovernmental entity (presumably to an entity like a third-party debt collector) by the "spouse, former spouse, child of the debtor, or such child's parent, legal guardian or responsible relative," the debt remains a domestic-support obligation.[41] In order to obtain a discharge, this first requirement is waived if the debtor executed a "written waiver of discharge" after the case was filed and the court approved it.[42]

There are no cases construing §1328(a) from the Southern District of Texas or the Fifth Circuit.[43] A problematic area in this first requirement is the provision that the debtor must certify that pre-petition domestic support obligations are paid, "but only to the extent provided for by the plan...."[44] How can this be if no part of a domestic-support obligation is dischargeable?[45] The answer lies in the interplay of §§1322(a)(2), 507(a)(1)(B) and 1322(a)(4).[46] Under those sections, if the assignee of a domestic support obligation—other than an assignee to whom the assignor assigns voluntarily "for the purpose of collecting the debt" —agrees to less than full payment of its claim and the plan provides that all of debtor's "projected disposable income" for five years will be

---

39   11 U.S.C. §104(14A)(B).
40   11 U.S.C. §101(14A)(C).
41   11 U.S.C. §101(14A)(D).
42   11 U.S.C. §1328.
43   *See In re Chapter 13 Fee Applications*, 2006 WL 2850115, 11-12 (Bankr. S.D. Tex. Oct. 3, 2006) (addendum showing contents of Debtor's Certification, Motion for Entry of Chapter 13 Discharge and Proposed Discharge Order).
44   11 U.S.C. §1328(a).
45   11 U.S.C. §1328(a)(2); 11 U.S.C. §523(a)(5).
46   William L. Norton, Jr., *Norton Bankruptcy Law and Practice* §153:2 (3d ed. 2008).

applied toward the plan, then the debtor may still receive a discharge even if such claims are not completely paid.[47] Those claims are still nondischargeable but they just do not have to be fully paid under the plan.[48] There are no cases so far construing §1328(a).

The second BAPCPA requirement (set forth in §1328(g)) is that the debtor complete an "instructional course concerning personal financial management" after the filing of the petition.[49] There are two exceptions to this requirement: (1) the debtor is a person described in §109(h)(4); or (2) the debtor resides in a district deemed without adequate instructional courses. Presently, there are no cases from the Southern District of Texas or Fifth Circuit construing §1328(g).

The first exception is if the court determines, after notice and hearing, that the debtor is unable to complete the course because of "incapacity, disability, or active military duty in a military combat zone."[50] Incapacity means mental illness or mental deficiency that renders the debtor unable to make rational decisions regarding his financial responsibilities.[51] Disability means physical impairment that renders the debtor unable with reasonable effort to be briefed in person or via telephone or Internet.[52]

In a chapter 7 case the court in the District of New Jersey held that the debtor who had died post-petition was exempt from the financial management course requirement because he was unable to participate, and such a course would not help him in the future anyway.[53] Specifically, in *In re Trembulak,* 362 B.R. 205 (Bankr. D. N.J. 2007), the court cogently held that:

> clearly the Debtor herein cannot participate in an instructional course on personal financial management and obviously such a course will not aid the Debtor in avoiding future financial distress. It seems palpably obvious that if a financial management course would

---

47   *Id.*

48   *Id.*

49   *See In re Fuller*, 2005 WL 3454699 (Bankr. W.D. Pa. Dec. 16, 2005) (holding that this course is distinct from the pre-bankruptcy counseling course, and the personal financial management course must be done after the petition is filed).

50   11 U.S.C. §109(h)(4).

51   *Id.*

52   *Id.*

53   *In re Trembulak*, 362 B.R. 205 (Bankr. D. N.J. 2007)

be meaningless for an 81-year-old, hearing-impaired debtor, suffering from prostate cancer, then such a course would likewise offer even less benefit to a deceased debtor.[54]

The second exception is if the debtor lives in a district in which the U.S. Trustee has determined that the courses are inadequate "to service the additional individuals who would otherwise be required to complete such instructional course by reason of the requirements of paragraph (1)."[55] There is currently no case law construing this second exception.

The third BAPCPA requirement is a finding by the court, after a notice and a hearing held not more than 10 days before the discharge order is entered, that "there is no reasonable cause to believe that" $522(q)(1)$ is applicable and there is no pending proceeding whereby the debtor may be found guilty of a felony (as described in $522(q)(1)(A)$) or liable for a debt (as described in $522(q)(1)(B)$).[56] There are no cases from the Southern District of Texas or the Fifth Circuit construing $1328(h)$.

Section $522(q)(1)(A)$ states that a debtor "may not exempt any amount of an interest in property" (real or personal property debtor or debtor's dependent uses as a residence; cooperative that owns property that debtor or debtor's dependent uses as a residence; burial plot for debtor or debtor's dependent; and real or personal property that debtor or debtor's dependent claims as a homestead) that "exceeds in the aggregate $125,000" if the debtor has been convicted of a felony. A felony is an "offense punishable by a maximum term of imprisonment of more than one year."[57] Section $522(q)(1)(A)$ has an additional requirement that the exemption limitation would be triggered if in light of the circumstances, such a debtor's filing demonstrates an abusive filing.

Section $522(q)(1)(B)$ limits a debtor's claim of exemptions in property (as listed in the above paragraph) if the debtor "owes a debt arising from": violations in federal and state securities law; fraud in a fiduciary capacity in the purchase or sale of securities; civil remedies under 11 U.S.C. 1964; or a "criminal act, intentional tort, or willful or reckless

---

54   *Id.* at 207.
55   11 U.S.C. $1328(g)(2)$.
56   11 U.S.C. $1328(h)$.
57   18 U.S.C. 3156.

misconduct" causing "serious physical injury or death" in the past five years.

There are no cases yet that discuss this third requirement, and commentary on this section has been rudimentary.[58] Nevertheless, before BAPCPA was effective, some commentators had already expressed confusion over the execution and implications of this subsection.[59] For example, the timing of the hearing, which has to be held no more than 10 days before the discharge order is entered, is "ridiculous."[60] The entry of a discharge order is not a date that is fixed, so counting that 10 days in reverse order is onerous.[61] Also, whether the debtor is able to claim an exemption that is greater than $125,000 for his property would have been determined in the early days of the chapter 13 case rather than just before the entry of discharge.[62]

The pending proceedings referred to in subsection 1328(h)(2) seem to contemplate very unlikely scenarios.[63] Those actions would have to be filed during the chapter 13 case or would have to be pending during the time the debtor makes his monthly chapter 13 plan payments.[64] Additionally, if the debtor does not claim an exemption in the stated property and there is an action pending as described in subsection 1328(h)(2), may a discharge be entered?[65] What if there is a pending action and the debtor does not seek to exempt property that exceeds $125,000?[66] Is this subsection meant to delay or bar entry of discharge for the debtor?[67] It remains to be seen as these issues make their way to the courts.

---

58   See, e.g., Jon Ann Giblin et al., *The 2005 Bankruptcy Reform Act*, 61 BUS. LAW. 949, 966 (2006) (discussing §1328(h)'s requirement that if reasonable ground exists that §522(q) action may be applicable or pending, court must delay entry of discharge until that action is concluded).

59   Keith Lundin & Henry Hildebrand, III, American Law Institute – American Bar Association Continuing Legal Education, Section-by-Section Analysis of Chapter 13 after BAPCPA 115 (2005).

60   *Id.*

61   *Id.*

62   *Id.*

63   *Id.*

64   *Id.*

65   *Id.*

66   *Id.*

67   *Id.*

I. Consumer Discharge

F. Effect of Audit Issues on Chapter 7 Discharges (§727(d)(4) on Revocation of Chapter 7 Discharge)

Section 727(d)(4) states that "on the request of the trustee, a creditor, or the United States Trustee, and after notice and hearing, the court shall revoke a discharge" if:

> The debtor has failed to explain satisfactorily—
>
> a material misstatement in an audit referred to in Section 586(f) of title 28; or
>
> a failure to make available for inspection all necessary accounts, papers, documents, financial records, files, and all other papers, things, or property belonging to the debtor that are requested for an audit referred to in Section 586(f) of title 28.

Section 586(f) of title 28 authorizes the U.S. Trustee for each district to use contract auditors to audit cases.[68] Those audits must be performed according to procedures set out in §603(a) of BAPCPA. Audits must be conducted by independent certified public accountants or licensed public accountants using "generally accepted auditing standards" or GAAS.

In brief, §586(f) of BAPCPA states that audits must "clearly and conspicuously . . . state material misstatement of income or expenditures or of assets." If there is a material misstatement reported, the clerk of the court must give notice to the creditors in the case. Additionally, if there is a material misstatement, the U.S. Trustee shall, if appropriate, report it to the U.S. Attorney, and also take appropriate steps including filing an adversary proceeding to revoke the debtor's discharge.[69]

Section 727(e) provides time limits within which the trustee, creditor or the U.S. Trustee may bring a revocation of discharge action under subsections (d)(1), (2) and (3), but provides none for §727(d)(4). Although the Bankruptcy Code is silent on that time limit, perhaps those parties may rely on "analogous" state or federal statutes of limitations.[70]

---

68 However, the U.S. Trustee Program temporarily suspended these audits in January 2008 due to budgetary constraints and resumed them to a limited extent in May 2008.

69 *See also* 18 U.S.C. §3057.

70 *See Lampf v. Gilbertson*, 501 U.S. 350 (1991).

Presently, there are only two cases that discuss §727(d)(4). One case is from the Bankruptcy Court in the Eastern District of New York. In *In re Ventura*, 375 B.R. 103 (Bankr. E.D.N.Y. 2007), the court held that cause existed to dismiss the debtor's chapter 7 case. The court stated that dismissal was appropriate where a debtor, after his case was randomly selected for audit, failed to fulfill the statutory duties of cooperating with the chapter 7 trustee and auditor, failed to surrender records to the chapter 7 trustee and auditor or failed to appear for examination, with the result that the trustee was unable to administer the case and the auditor was unable to conduct the audit. In that case, the U.S. Trustee moved to dismiss the debtor's case after the debtor failed, among other transgressions, to cooperate with the firm conducting the random audit.[71] The U.S. Trustee filed a motion to dismiss the case pursuant to §707(a) and to bar the debtor from filing another chapter 7 case for a year.[72] Although the debtor had not received a discharge, the U.S. Trustee argued that since Congress contemplated a very harsh remedy – revocation of discharge – for a debtor's failure to cooperate with a random audit, it implies that Congress would approve of prohibitions on the debtor's ability to file another case if the debtor fails to cooperate.[73] The court disagreed with the U.S. Trustee's position and cited to several sections of the Code that show that Congress knows how to impose prohibitions and limitations against debtors under very specific circumstances.[74] With BAPCPA, Congress enacted a new subsection to allow for revocation of discharge in the event of the debtor's noncooperation in a random audit.[75] Moreover, §109, which lists eligibility requirements for a debtor, does not include a subsection that bars a debtor's ability to file a subsequent case for failure to cooperate in a random audit.[76] The court did not close the door completely on imposing a temporary bar against filing a new case if the debtor "engaged in egregious conduct" or a "scheme to hinder his creditors."[77] Hence, if the debtor acts fraudulently in connection with his random audit, this court believed that barring that debtor from a

---

71 *In re Ventura*, 375 B.R. 103 (Bankr. E.D.N.Y. 2007).
72 *Id.* at 104.
73 *Id.* at 110.
74 *Id.* at 111.
75 *Id.*
76 *Id.*
77 *Id.* at 112.

subsequent filing for a period of time, while not specifically provided for by the Code, would be within the court's discretionary powers.[78]

The other case is from the Southern District of Georgia. In *In re Kelton*, 389 B.R. 812 (Bankr. S.D. Ga. 2008), the auditor reported a material misstatement because the chapter 13 debtor understated his current monthly income on the means test form by $1,204.88. The debtor moved to strike the report, arguing that the report was erroneous and that, alternatively, any misstatement was not material. After taking testimony and confirming that the finding was not erroneous, the court held that the misstatement was material even though the debtor's disposable income would still be negative with the upward adjustment to current monthly income. The court stated that "[a]ccurate disclosure of a debtor's financial situation is perhaps the primary duty of debtors seeking relief under the Bankruptcy Code." *Id.* at 818. Further, this was the "exact situation the audit system was designed to discover." *Id.* at 819.

---

78   *Id.* at 111.

I. Consumer Discharge

II.

Attorneys' Fees
in Chapter 13 Cases

A key area of interest for any attorney practicing in the chapter 13 area is getting paid. Specifically, practitioners are interested in which professionals may be entitled to payment in a case, when may they get paid and how much they are entitled to receive. For example, in *In re Bellamy,* 379 B.R. 86 (Bankr. D. Md. 2007), the court held:

> After examining Section 1326(b) and the cases which have interpreted it, this court reaches the conclusion that the statute does require the Trustee to pay in full any allowed and outstanding administrative claim [including attorney fees] as a part of any distribution, before distributions may be made to other claimants, except possibly holders of domestic support obligations entitled to priority under Section 507(a)(1).

However, in *In re Bernales,* 345 B.R. 206 (Bankr. C.D. Cal. 2006), the court held that the payment provisions embodied in the Bankruptcy Code and under local standing orders did not preempt state law on the unauthorized practice of law. Thus, the court observed that a bankruptcy petition preparer (BPP) engaged in the unauthorized practice of law by advising its debtor-client in an e-mail message that most bankruptcy courts allowed debtors to pay filing fees in installments. The court imposed sanctions against the BPP by ordering the disgorgement of any compensation received, fining the BPP $2,000 to the debtor and to U.S. Trustee, and permanently enjoining the BPP from preparing petitions in the Central District of California.

A. Paying Debtor's Counsel

1. Cautionary Tales

It has long been established that the attorney for a chapter 7 debtor does not get paid from the assets of the bankruptcy estate. Thus, once a case converts to chapter 7, whether it be from chapter 11, chapter 12 or chapter 13, the attorney generally is no longer entitled to be paid from the assets of the estate because his/her client is no longer empowered to act as a trustee for the estate. This point is brought home with some force in *In re Montemayor Trucking Inc.*, 2006 WL 3545459 (Bankr. S.D. Tex. Dec. 18, 2006). In that case, the court stated:

> A debtor's attorney will be entitled to attorneys' fees that will be paid as an administrative expense in only two circumstances: (1) if the debtor is a debtor-in-possession in chapter 11 and therefore exercises the authority of a trustee, and (2) if the case is a chapter 12 or a chapter 13 case. There is no other provision in the Bankruptcy Code for allowance of fees for a debtor's attorney. Therefore . . . applicant is not entitled to an award of attorneys' fees for services rendered subsequent to the date that the case was converted [from Chapter 11 to Chapter 7] and his client, the Debtor, ceased to exercise the authority of a trustee.

Additionally, at least one court has upheld the practice whereby court-imposed sanctions ordered in one bankruptcy case may be paid from fees otherwise payable in another case. Thus, in *In re Smith*, 2006 WL 3627149 (8th Cir. Dec. 14, 2006), the Eighth Circuit held that a bankruptcy court's order instructing the trustee to withhold attorney's fees in other bankruptcy cases as sanctions for the attorney's continued violation of an earlier court order was a proper exercise of the court's discretion.

2. How Much Is Enough for a Chapter 13 Case?

Many, if not most, jurisdictions have local rules or orders determining how much an attorney for the debtor can be paid in a chapter 13 case without seeking special approval of fees. After the enactment of BAPCPA, the complexity of filing any consumer case increased. Thus, most courts have also increased the allowed payment. The Southern District of Texas is no exception. In *In re Chapter 13 Fee Applications*, 2006 WL 2850115 (Bankr. S.D. Tex. Oct. 3, 2006), the Bankruptcy Court of the Southern District of Texas entered such an order increasing the fixed fee amount of chapter 13 attorneys' fees. That order provides:

> The maximum fixed fee for chapter 13 cases filed after entry of this Order is $3,085.00, including all expenses other than the filing fee. For cases dismissed before confirmation or within 120 days after confirmation, the maximum fixed fee is $2,700.00.

Other jurisdictions take slightly different approaches from that embraced by the Southern District of Texas. Fixed attorney's fee amounts, however, in a chapter 13 case tend to range from $2,500 to $3,750. In the District of Colorado, the presumptively reasonable fee is $3,000. *See, e.g., In re Murray,* 348 B.R. 917 (Bankr. M.D. Ga. 2006) ("Administrative Order of January 3, 2005, shall be amended to reflect the following changes: Effective as to cases filed on or after August 1, 2006, an attorney for a Chapter 13 debtor or joint debtors . . . need not file an initial fee application if the fee sought to be paid per case is $2,500.00 or less"); *In re Mayer,* 2006 WL 2850451 (Bankr. D. Kan. Oct. 2, 2006) (District of Kansas has increased presumptive attorney fee amount, concluding that "the increased workload and responsibilities of lawyers filing chapter 13 cases in the wake of BAPCPA merit an increase in the presumptive fee from $2,000 to $2,500."); *In re McNally,* 2006 WL 2348687 (Bankr. D. Colo. Aug. 10, 2006) ("In this District, we have determined the Presumptively Reasonable Fee structure is a more efficient and effective procedure than examining the intricacies of every case. Our current process has worked well, but will need tweaking, both as a result of BAPCPA and possibly some based on our collective experience of working under it for a few years. These things are still a work-in-process."); *In re Mullings,* 2006 WL 2130648 (Bankr. E.D. Okla. July 26, 2006) ("Effective August 15, 2006, in all cases filed or converted to a case under Chapter 13 of the Bankruptcy Code, the presumptive attorney fee shall be $3,750.00 in individual and small business cases. This will not eliminate the necessity of attorneys to continue to keep contemporaneous time records that identify the work performed. In some situations the Court will still consider reduction or disgorgement of fees when the professional work does not meet the high standards set by this Court. Upon proper application, the Court may consider enhancement of fees above the presumptive fee.").

Fee enhancements above the presumptive fee structure may occur but must be based on the facts and circumstances of each individual case. Enhancements may be warranted because of the complexity of the case itself, the need to litigate bankruptcy related matters, or the like. For example, in *In re Eliapo*, 468 F.3d 592 (9th Cir. 2006), the Ninth Circuit addressed the issue of whether the attorney for the chapter 13 debtors was entitled to compensation for work involving the debtors' vehicle loan. The Ninth Circuit was careful to note that any fee enhancement depended upon the factual record. Unfortunately, according to the Ninth Circuit, the record on appeal had not been fully developed; therefore, the issue, which was not raised before the bankruptcy appellate panel (BAP), did not fall within the "exceptional circumstance" exception to the general rule providing for the waiver of an issue not raised before the BAP and was waived for purposes of further review by the Ninth Circuit on the attorney's appeal challenging the denial of requested enhanced compensation.

3. When Do I Get Paid?

The question of when an attorney in a chapter 13 case is entitled to payment is an important one. Bankruptcy practitioners are intimately aware of the adage "time is money." In *In re Erwin*, 376 B.R. 897 (Bankr. C.D. Ill. 2007), the court held that the equal payment provision, directed at debtors and not chapter 13 trustees, does not require a trustee's monthly payments to secured creditors to be perfectly equal in amount. Thus, trustees may continue to pay the debtors' attorney's fees on an accelerated basis despite the resulting increase in secured creditor payments once the attorney is fully paid. The possibility of accelerating fees, however, is tempered by other chapter 13 realities.

In *In re DeSardi*, 340 B.R. 790 (Bankr. S.D. Tex. 2006), several creditors that provided purchase-money financing and obtained security interests in vehicles acquired by chapter 13 debtors for their personal use objected to the treatment of their claims in the debtors' proposed chapter 13 plans. In that case, the court held that administrative expenses in the form of adequate-protection payments to such creditors out-ranked a debtor's attorney's fees based on protections found in §507(b), and sustained the creditors' objections. This decision is supported by in *In re Dispirito,* 371 B.R. 695 (Bankr. D. N.J. 2007), where the court warned that adequate-protection payments to automobile lenders may have priority over claims for attorneys' fees made by counsel for chapter 13 debtors.

4. Exception from Discharge

What happens in the situation where a debtor agrees to pay post-confirmation attorney's fees outside of a plan and then breaches that promise? In *In re Johnson, 344 B.R. 104* (B.A.P. 9th Cir. 2006), the court held that a chapter 13 debtor's obligation for the post-confirmation fees of his bankruptcy counsel would not be discharged pursuant to his performance under the chapter 13 plan. The court reasoned that a chapter 13 debtor's obligation for the post-confirmation fees of his bankruptcy counsel would not be discharged upon the completion of the debtor's payments under the plan and the entry of an order of discharge at least where the plan contained a provision that supported the performance by the debtor of post-discharge obligations. In this case, the debtor's confirmed plan specifically provided that such post-confirmation fees would be paid by the debtor directly and would not be discharged upon the entry of an order of discharge. This plan provision, which enabled the debtor to complete his plan payments without reducing or stretching out payments to other creditors, was not inconsistent with any provision of the Bankruptcy Code, according to the court. Note, however, that generally courts hold that prepetition attorney's fees are dischargeable.

B. Paying Creditors' Counsel

The question of paying creditors' attorneys' fees poses several challenging issues. Initially, the cases may be roughly divided into two camps: (1) cases involving mortgages (including the primary home mortgage); and (2) all other cases. In *In re Ryker,* 2007 WL 2138590 (3d Cir. July 27, 2007), the court articulated the general approach. In that case, state law provided and the Bankruptcy Code generally recognized that the mortgage company's attorneys' fees in connection with the enforcement of the mortgage may be shifted to the debtor for collection and payment. Thus, the Third Circuit held that several mortgage-holders were entitled to attorneys' fees incurred in connection with the sale of commercial property upon which the chapter 13 debtor defaulted.

In *In re Padilla*, 379 B.R. 643 (Bankr. S.D. Tex. 2007), in a series of consolidated cases, a number of chapter 13 debtors challenged certain fees and expenses charged by home mortgage lenders where the lenders failed to file reimbursement applications with the bankruptcy court. According to the court, these lenders failed to comply with Federal Rule of Bankruptcy Procedure 2016(a). That Rule governs the collection of reimbursable fees and expenses from the bankruptcy estate. In these cases, the court held that the failure to comply with Rule 2016(a) or the imposition of reimbursable expenses beyond those allowed by contract and applicable nonbankruptcy law pre-petition not only violated the rule but also violated the order confirming the chapter 13 cases, entitling the debtors to relief against the creditors, including costs and fees. This is reinforced by the court's decision in *In re Murphy*, 346 B.R. 79 (Bankr. S.D.N.Y. 2006). The court reminded practitioners that it does not serve to simply provide comfort orders to parties in interest and that certain procedures must be followed in seeking an award of fees. In this case, the court stated that, notwithstanding the *ex parte* application by the mortgagee for a "comfort order" that would find that the temporary stay arising in a chapter 13 case filed by a repeat filer had terminated 30 days after order for relief, the bankruptcy court's institutional function was limited to finding an objective fact, that is, that the stay had in fact terminated pursuant to the new provision in BAPCPA. Furthermore, the court admonished the attorney that a request for fees, even in conjunction with the "comfort order" request, must be filed and noticed provided in accordance with the Federal Rules of Bankruptcy Procedure.

In re Hudson, 2007 WL 4219421 (Bankr. C.D. Ill. Nov. 27, 2007), provides a good example of the treatment of attorneys' fees in the nonmortgage context. In that case, the court stated that the attorney's fees that the debtor was ordered to pay, and that were incurred in a paternity/support proceeding, were nondischargeable because they were considered in the nature of support. In essence, the court adopted a variant of the "equal-dignity" rule, that is, fees incurred to assert a right to the nondischargeability of a claim are entitled to equal treatment.

II. Attorneys' Fees in Chapter 13 Cases

Credit Counseling
and Debtor Education

Section 109(h)(1) of the Bankruptcy Code, a BAPCPA provision, requires that an individual debtor filing under any chapter of the Bankruptcy Code receive an individual or group briefing outlining the opportunities for available credit counseling and providing assistance in performing a budget analysis during the 180 days preceding the filing date. The individual must receive such a briefing from an approved nonprofit budget and credit counseling agency as described in §111(a) of the Bankruptcy Code. The statute does not mandate that the counseling be in person; rather, the statute allows counseling to be conducted, for example, by telephone or on the Internet.

Pursuant to §111(a), the clerks of the bankruptcy courts must maintain publicly-available lists of the credit counseling agencies approved by the U.S. Trustee. The U.S. Trustees approve the agencies, and §111 sets forth the requirements for such approval, as well as other relevant provisions. Many clerks simply provide a link to the Web site of the U.S. Trustee Program where one may search for approved credit counseling agencies by states and districts.[79] The link is: http://www.usdoj.gov/ust/eo/bapcpa/ccde/cc_approved.htm. In July 2006, the Code of Federal

---

79   In addition to the name of the agency, on its Web site the U.S. Trustee Program includes the agency's address, its phone number, how the agency offers the services (for example, in person, telephone, Internet), the languages in which the agency offers the services and other pertinent information.

Regulations published the U.S. Trustee Program's interim final rule regarding credit counseling at 28 C.F.R. §§58.15, 58.16 and 58.17. These sections address criteria for approval as a provider, procedures to be included on the approved list, denial or removal as a provider, and other relevant information. The comment period on the proposed final rule, which included some significant changes to the interim rule, closed on April 1, 2008.[80]

Does this counseling requirement apply in the situation where an involuntary bankruptcy case is commenced against an individual debtor? In *In re Allen*, 378 B.R. 151 (Bankr. N.D. Tex. 2007), the court answered no. The court stated that the credit-counseling requirement added by BAPCPA pertains only to an individual who is the subject of a voluntary bankruptcy case and does not apply to putative debtors who are the subject of involuntary petitions. The court in *In re Diloreto,* 2008 WL 141922 (Bankr. E.D. Pa. Jan. 11, 2008), reached the same conclusion, holding that "the express language of section 109(h)(1) makes clear that the credit counseling requirement applies only to voluntary petitions." The court observed, however, that a pass on credit counseling is not tantamount to a pass on the Federal Rules of Bankruptcy Procedure. The court rejected the petitioning creditors' argument that delivery of the involuntary petition by Federal Express constituted delivery by regular mail and granted the debtor's request for a dismissal, adding that:

> the petitioning creditor here did not comply with the service requirements of Rule 7004 when Federal Express delivered the involuntary petition to the putative debtor.

A. Curriculum

An obvious threshold issue that must be addressed when considering the credit counseling requirements is determining what information the counseling is designed to provide to the debtor. The Bankruptcy Code provides little assistance with the requirements for the curriculum for credit counseling. Section 109(h)(1) simply states that the session must outline the "opportunities for available credit counseling" and assist the

---

80 The interim rule remained in effect as of the printing of this book.

person in "performing a related budget analysis." Section 111(c)(2)(E) states that an approved credit counseling agency must, at a minimum:

> provide adequate counseling with respect to a client's credit problems that includes an analysis of such client's current financial condition, factors that caused such financial condition, and how such client can develop a plan to respond to the problems without incurring negative amortization of debt.

The Department of Justice Interim Final Rule, found at 28 C.F.R. §58.15, which is presently in effect, provides a little additional guidance. Subsection (f)(1) states that the counselors may not provide legal advice, but they shall:

> [P]rovide adequate briefings, budget analysis, and credit counseling services to clients lasting an average of 60 to 90 minutes in length that include an outline of available counseling opportunities to resolve a client's credit problems, an analysis of the client's current financial condition, discussion of the factors that caused such financial condition, and assistance in developing a plan to respond to the client's problems without incurring negative amortization of debt . . . .

The U.S. Trustee Program's form application to become an approved credit counseling agency states these same requirements in the accompanying instructions. Further, Appendix A to the application requires the applicant to certify that it will meet these requirements.

The comment period regarding the proposed Department of Justice Final Rule, which will replace the above when it becomes effective, ended on April 1, 2008. This proposed rule addressed the curriculum with a little more specificity. In draft 28 C.F.R. §58.19, it states that an agency must "[p]rovide adequate counseling to its clients" in order to become an approved agency. Draft 28 C.F.R. §58.12(b)(3) defines "adequate counseling" as:

> the actual receipt by a client from an approved agency of all counseling services, and all other applicable services, rights, and protections specified in:
>
> (i) 11 U.S.C. §109(h)(1);
>
> (ii) 11 U.S.C. §111; and
>
> (iii) this rule . . . .

Section 58.12(b)(12) then defines "counseling services" as:

> all counseling required by 11 U.S.C. §§109(h) and 111, and this rule including, without limitation, services that are typically of at least 60 minutes in duration and that shall at a minimum include:

> (i) Performing on behalf of, and providing to, each client a written analysis of each client's current financial condition, which analysis shall include a budget analysis, consideration of all alternatives to resolve a client's credit problems, discussion of the factors that caused such financial condition, and identification of all methods by which the client can develop a plan to respond to the financial problems without incurring negative amortization of debt; and

> (ii) Providing each client the opportunity to have the agency negotiate an alternative payment schedule with regard to each unsecured consumer debt under terms as set forth in 11 U.S.C §502(k) or, if the client accepts this option and the agency is unable to provide this service, the agency shall refer the client to another approved agency in the appropriate federal district that provides it.

B. Issues Relating to Timing of Counseling

The timing of the credit counseling requirement presents several areas for litigation, which are addressed in turn.

1. Within 180 Days

A plain reading of the provision appears to give little relief to the debtor who waits too long between receiving credit counseling and filing a petition for relief or, for that matter, little flexibility to the courts.[81] Thus, the court in *In re Gaddis,* 2007 WL 1610783 (Bankr. D. Kan. June 4, 2007), held that a debtor receiving credit counseling 186 days before filing the bankruptcy petition simply did not satisfy §109(h). Moreover, *In re Dyer,* 381 B.R. 200 (Bankr. W.D.N.C. 2007), stands for the sensible proposition that the general equitable powers of the bankruptcy court will not save a failure to adhere to the pre-filing counseling requirements. In that case, the court held that a chapter 7 case filed by debtors who had obtained credit counseling more than 180

---

81   *In re Giles,* 361 B.R. 212 (Bankr. D. Utah 2007); *In re Williams,* 359 B.R. 590 (Bankr. E.D.N.C. 2007)

days prepetition had to be dismissed based on the debtors' ineligibility to be bankruptcy debtors, notwithstanding the power of the court generally to invoke §105 to enter any "necessary or appropriate" orders or equitable doctrines. Thus, the §105 power could not be used as a "trump" to override §109's "credit counseling" requirement. In *In re Giles*, 361 B.R. 212 (Bankr. D. Utah 2007), the court further rejected the notion that substantial compliance should suffice. In *Giles*, the debtors obtained credit counseling 182 days prior to commencement of their chapter 13 case. Doing the math, the court found that they had failed to satisfy their prefiling obligation. Thus, the court stated that it had no discretion to excuse the debtors' noncompliance on the theory that they had complied with the spirit of the credit counseling requirement. Therefore, the court granted the trustee's motion to dismiss. Consistent with this result is *In re Williams*, 359 B.R. 590 (Bankr. E.D.N.C. 2007). In *Williams*, the court found that:

> Section 109(h) does provide several exceptions for debtors who are unable to complete their credit counseling for various reasons prior to their filing. However, it does not provide an alternative for those who complete their credit counseling more than 180 days prior to their filing.

One court developed a little flexibility by calling the counseling "ongoing" where the debtor continued to attempt to comply with the budget provided in counseling. The ongoing nature of the counseling extended the session so that the required time period was satisfied. Thus, in *In re Bricksin*, 346 B.R. 497 (Bankr. N.D. Cal. 2006), the court determined that although the debtors' initial credit counseling session, occurring more than 180 days prior to petition date, was insufficient to satisfy the credit counseling requirement, the debtors' conduct, after they obtained this initial counseling, in participating in and performing under the repayment plan developed by the credit counselor for several months until they were eventually forced to file a bankruptcy petition, as their counselor had initially recommended, qualified as ongoing "credit counseling" that extended the counseling into the statutory 180-day period, thus satisfying the requirements.

Other courts have found a little flexibility where the mistake was the attorney's rather than the debtor's. In *In re Enloe*, 373 B.R. 123 (Bankr. D. Colo. 2007), the court found that the mere fact that the debtors, as a result of their attorney's error, did not file for chapter 7 relief until 189 days after they received credit counseling did not warrant the dismissal of the case. The case seems to suggest that attorney mistake may constitute some form of "excusable neglect," at least where a debtor did undertake some form of counseling before the petition date.

In *In re Hess*, 347 B.R. 489 (Bankr. D. Vt. 2006), the court expanded the exercise of discretion in assessing the remedy for noncompliance under §109(h). In *Hess*, the court found that the mere fact that the debtors, because of their inability to provide required proof of prepetition credit counseling or to qualify for an express waiver or exemption, were ineligible for bankruptcy relief did not necessarily mean that the court had to dismiss their petitions. In that case, one debtor checked the box on the petition indicating that he had obtained the requisite prepetition credit counseling but was unable to provide a certificate from the credit counseling agency because the agency was not an approved agency at the relevant time. Moreover, the court found that the chapter 7 case filed by the other debtor was mistakenly filed, while her attorney was absent from the law office to undergo an emergency medical procedure, before the debtor could obtain prepetition credit counseling. In refusing to dismiss the petition, the court held that "[u]nder the totality of the circumstances presented, [the Court] has discretion to allow the cases to proceed, notwithstanding the procedural eligibility defect."

In yet another permutation of possible facts, a court exercised its discretion where the court found that the debtor filed post-BAPCPA, but got counseling before §109(h) became effective. In *In re Meza*, 2007 WL 1821416 (E.D. Cal. June 25, 2007), the court found that the debtor's bankruptcy petition substantially complied with the eligibility requirements of §109(h) despite the debtor receiving credit counseling prior to enactment of the BAPCPA and filing the petition after BAPCPA's enactment.

2. Repeat Filers

As stated above, §109(h)(1) requires a debtor to obtain the credit counseling during the 180 days preceding the filing date. There do not appear to be any published cases addressing this requirement with respect to "repeat filers." Based on the plain language of the statute, however, one can assume that a repeat filer's fulfillment of the credit counseling requirement with respect to a prior case carries over to a subsequent case only if he files the subsequent case within 180 days of obtaining the original counseling. Thus, it appears that a repeat filer must retake the counseling course to be eligible to file a subsequent case if more than 180 days has passed between the counseling and the subsequent repeat filing.

3. Counseling on the Petition Date

Neither the Southern District of Texas nor the Fifth Circuit have addressed the law exam-like question of whether the debtor can receive credit counseling and then file his petition on the same day. Although the better-reasoned approach appears to be that the requirement is about sequence rather than date (thus, so long as the debtor receives the counseling prior in time to filing the petition, it may be received on the same date as the petition date), there does appear to be a number of cases that hold otherwise.

a. Must Be at Least One Day Prior to Petition Date

In *In re Francisco,* 386 B.R. 854 (Bankr. D. N.M. 2008), *rev'd,* 390 B.R. 700 (B.A.P. 10th Cir. 2008), the bankruptcy court held that a debtor must obtain the budget and credit counseling prior to the day of the filing of the petition and concluded that the proper remedy was to dismiss, and not strike, the petition, an issue taken up later in this book. The Tenth Circuit Bankruptcy Appellate Panel reversed the bankruptcy court, however, holding that a debtor satisfies the credit counseling requirement when he obtains it on the same day as, but prior to, the filing of the bankruptcy petition.

In *In re Gossett,* 369 B.R. 361 (Bankr. N.D. Ill. 2007), the court held that the debtor who obtained the required prepetition credit counseling briefing on the same day as the date of filing bankruptcy does not comply with the statutory directive that he or she obtained a briefing "during the 180-day period preceding the date of filing of the petition" and, therefore, is not eligible to be a debtor under the Bankruptcy Code. Moreover, in *In re Cole,* 347 B.R. 70 (Bankr. E.D. Tenn. 2006), the court held that in specifying that the debtor must obtain credit counseling during the 180-day period "preceding the date" that the petition was filed, Congress plainly precluded debtors from filing for bankruptcy on the same date that credit counseling was obtained. In *In re Murphy,* 342 B.R. 671 (Bankr. D. D.C. 2006), the court held that to meet the requirements of §109(h), the debtor must receive the credit counseling at least the day before the filing, not on the date of the filing. In *In re Mills,* 341 B.R. 106 (Bankr. D. D.C. 2006), *abrogated by In re Barbaran,* 365 B.R. 333 (Bankr. D. D.C. 2007), the bankruptcy court reaffirmed its prior holding in *Murphy,* holding that under §109(h), the debtor must obtain credit counseling not just some hours, minutes or seconds prior to filing his petition, but at least one calendar day prior to the petition date. However, in *Barbaran* the court rejected its prior ruling in *Mills,* stating that the use of the term "date" in §109(h) represents the moment of the filing of the petition.

b. Counseling May Be Received on Petition Date

Addressing an issue of apparent first impression for the court, the Bankruptcy Appellate Panel for the Tenth Circuit has held that under BAPCPA an individual qualifies as a debtor so long as he or she completes the required credit counseling at any time between 180 days before, and the moment of, filing the bankruptcy petition. *See In re Francisco,* 390 B.R. 700 (B.A.P. 10th Cir. 2008). The panel thus reversed the decision of the bankruptcy court, which had held that the debtor must complete the credit counseling at the latest on the calendar day prior to the day of filing the petition. In so ruling, the panel recognized a split of authority and commented that both lines of cases were inherently sound. However, the panel stated that it was more persuaded by the reasoning of the "bright line" cases, which properly focused not on whether a debtor obtained his or her credit counseling within the 180-day period but, rather, on whether he or she obtained it by the statutorily-imposed deadline. Nothing in the legislative history supported an interpretation of that deadline as including a waiting period prior to the filing of the petition, the panel explained, and enforcing such a waiting period under the current statutory language would be difficult.

In *In re Moore,* 359 B.R. 665 (Bankr. E.D. Tenn. 2006), the court held that §109(h)(1) requires a debtor to receive a credit counseling briefing prior to the moment of filing the petition, so long as the 180-day outside limit is otherwise met. According to the court, §109(h)(1) governs not the period of time for doing an act after a bankruptcy case is commence, but rather describes the requisite time for taking a step to establish eligibility to file a case in the first instance, much like the time for filing a complaint to satisfy a statute of limitations. In *In re Spears,* 355 B.R. 116 (Bankr. E.D. Wis. 2006), the court held that the debtor who obtained credit counseling prior to, but on the same day as, the filing of her bankruptcy petition satisfied the requirement imposed by §109(h). Moreover, in *In re Hudson,* 352 B.R. 391 (Bankr. D. Md. 2006), the court held that a chapter 13 debtor who obtained credit counseling on the same day as filing his bankruptcy petition, but prior to the filing of his petition, nonetheless satisfied the statutory requirement that he obtain such counseling "during the 180-day period preceding the date of filing of the petition." In *In re Warren,* 339 B.R. 475 (Bankr. E.D. Ark. 2006), the court held that the requirement that the putative debtor obtain credit counseling prior to filing referred not just to the calendar date on which the petition was filed, but to the particular year, month, date and time of day of filing the petition, so as to require only that credit counseling precede the filing of the petition, not that it precede it by at least one calendar date. Additionally, in *In re Swanson,* 2006 WL 3782906 (Bankr. D. Idaho Dec. 21, 2006), the court held that the term "date of filing" as found in §109(h) referred to the specific calendar day and time the petition was filed. Here, the credit counseling the debtor obtained prior to the filing but on the same day he filed his bankruptcy petition complied with §109(h). Finally, in *In re Toccaline,* 2006 WL 2081517 (Bankr. D. Conn. July 17, 2006), the court found that credit counseling on the day of the filing was sufficient to meet the requirements of 11 U.S.C. §109(h)(1).

C. Preliminary Questions on Eligibility

1. Is Credit Counseling a Jurisdictional Issue?

When determining whether a debtor who has not complied with the specifications of §109 and who is seeking some form of exception, extension or exemption, the first question many courts have asked is: Is debtor eligibility a jurisdictional question? The majority of courts has determined that it is not a jurisdictional question, recasting the question as one of whether or not a debtor is eligible, an initial question that the bankruptcy court must address.

a. Not Jurisdictional

The majority of cases has concluded that the §109(h) counseling requirement is an eligibility and not jurisdictional issue. *In In re Mendez,* 367 B.R. 109 (B.A.P. 9th Cir. 2007), the court held that pre-bankruptcy credit counseling is not a jurisdictional prerequisite but, instead, is a matter of individual eligibility, subject to principles of waiver and estoppel. Consistent with *Mendez,* the court in *In re Hoshan,* 2008 WL 81994 (E.D. Pa. Jan. 7, 2008), held that the credit counseling requirement is not jurisdictional. Moreover, in *Warren v. Wirum,* 378 B.R. 640 (N.D. Cal. 2007), the district court determined that the credit counseling requirement was not jurisdictional in nature. Furthermore, in *Clippard v. Bass,* 365 B.R. 131 (W.D. Tenn. 2007), the court held that eligibility to be a debtor is not jurisdictional, and until the bankruptcy court determines eligibility, a bankruptcy case filed by an ineligible debtor actually exists, which cannot thereafter be deemed a nullity by simply striking the case as if it never existed. See subsequent discussion of strike vs. dismissal.

In two cases, the courts employed an extended analysis of the nonjurisdictional nature of §109(h) and, therefore, the appropriateness of the remedy of dismissal. In the first case, *In re Manalad,* 360 B.R. 288 (Bankr. C.D. Cal. 2007), the court found that the credit counseling requirement was not jurisdictional in nature and did not necessarily mandate dismissal. In rejecting a *per se* rule, the court articulated a multi-factor test for guiding its discretion. In determining whether a petition should be dismissed for failure to comply with the counseling requirements under §109(h), a court should consider the following factors: (1) whether the debtor has a reasonable explanation for not participating in budget and credit counseling within 180 days prior to filing bankruptcy petition; (2) whether the debtor participates in budget and credit counseling once the debtor learns that it is necessary;

and (3) whether it is determined, at a budget and credit counseling session, that the debtor's debts could not have been paid outside of bankruptcy.

In the second case, *In re Seaman,* 340 B.R. 698 (Bankr. E.D.N.Y. 2006), the court held that eligibility issues are not jurisdictional. The court determined that the appropriate remedy for failure to obtain credit counseling was dismissal rather than striking the petition because until the eligibility is determined, the case proceeds and thus cannot be a nullity. Further, the court stated, dismissal is appropriate because "[d]ismissal is the result in nearly all of the cases filed by petitioners who are ineligible under other subsections of Section 109."[82]

b. Jurisdictional

In *In re Giles*, 361 B.R. 212 (Bankr. D. Utah 2007), the court held that it lacked jurisdiction over the debtor's case where the debtor failed to comply with the credit counseling requirement imposed by §109(h). Moreover, in *In re Valdez*, 335 B.R. 801 (Bankr. S.D. Fla. 2005), the court held that where the petitioner was ineligible for failure to obtain credit counseling and failed to meet the standards for a waiver, the status of "debtor" was never conveyed. Finding eligibility to be jurisdictional, the court would "not consider this a dismissed case in which the individual was the debtor, for the purposes of denying the imposition of the automatic stay in subsequently filed case."

2. Does the Filing by an Ineligible Debtor Give Rise to the Automatic Stay?

After determining whether or not the filing by an ineligible debtor gives rise to a case the court has jurisdiction to hear, the next question the court must address is whether the automatic stay is triggered by the filing of a case by an ineligible debtor. The Southern District of Texas, in *In re Salazar*, 339 B.R. 622 (Bankr. S.D. Tex. 2006), determined that the filing by an ineligible debtor did not give rise to a bankruptcy case pending a determination on eligibility, and thus no protections

---

82   *See also Warren v. Wirum,* 378 B.R. 640 (N.D. Cal. 2007) (pre-petition credit counseling requirement is not jurisdictional); *In re Dyer,* 381 B.R. 200 (Bankr. W.D.N.C. 2007) ("credit counseling" requirement imposed by BAPCPA is not jurisdictional).

were available from the automatic stay. Thus, where the putative debtor filed a petition but was not eligible for bankruptcy relief because of a failure to obtain credit counseling, such filing did not give rise to a bankruptcy case or entitle a debtor, even temporarily until eligibility determination was made, to the protection of the automatic stay.

a. No Stay Implicated

In addition to *In re Salazar,* the bankruptcy court, in *In re Elmendorf,* 345 B.R. 486 (Bankr. S.D.N.Y. 2006), found that the filing of a bankruptcy petition without first obtaining credit counseling, which renders the debtor ineligible for bankruptcy relief, does not trigger the protection of the automatic stay. However, the court held that a bankruptcy court may decide, on a case-by-case basis, whether to strike the petition filed in violation of the credit counseling requirement.

b. Stay Implicated

In *In re Brown,* 342 B.R. 248 (Bankr. D. Md. 2006), the court held that the filing of a chapter 13 petition by the debtor who, as result of her failure to obtain credit counseling prepetition or to file a certification of exigent circumstances that was satisfactory to the court, was not eligible for chapter 13 relief was not a mere nullity, but gave rise to the automatic stay that remained in effect until the bankruptcy court denied the debtor's request for a waiver of the prepetition credit counseling requirement and dismissed the case. Moreover, in *In re Hawkins,* 340 B.R. 642 (Bankr. D. D.C. 2006), the court held that §362(b)(21) must be read as implying that the automatic stay was in effect while the court makes the threshold determination of jurisdiction. Thus, a petition by an ineligible debtor gives rise to a case in this limited sense and to an automatic stay until the case is dismissed. According to the court, §362 must be read as giving rise to an automatic stay when a petition is asserted to be filed under §§301, 302 or 303.

D. Strike or Dismiss, That Is the Question

The next question the court must address is what to do with a case filed by an ineligible debtor. Some courts say strike the petition; others may dismiss the case. The Southern District of Texas, in *Wyttenbach v. C.I.R.,* 382 B.R. 726 (S.D. Tex. 2008), determined that the appropriate remedy was to strike the petition because no case was validly commenced. There, the court held that striking the petition and retroactively annulling the automatic stay was a permissible remedy for an individual's noncompliance with the credit counseling requirement. Likewise, in *In re Hubbard,* 333 B.R. 377 (Bankr. S.D. Tex. 2005), because the court determined that the debtors were ineligible, and thus no case was commenced, the court found that the appropriate remedy for their ineligibility was to strike their petitions rather than dismiss their cases. Other courts, however, have found that when the petition is filed, the case is commenced and thus, the remedy requires dismissal for cause.

At first blush, this would seem to be a distinction without a difference. However, if the case is dismissed for cause rather than the petition simply struck as *void ab initio,* the debtor's future protection from the automatic stay is limited by §362(c)(3). That provision, as revised by BAPCPA, renders a petition filed within one year of the dismissal of another bankruptcy case presumptively filed in bad faith and, thus, limits the automatic stay to 30 days.[83] This new provision is triggered by the dismissal of a petition and not by the striking of a petition. Though this presumption can be rebutted, it is not a desirable way to begin a bankruptcy case.

1. Strike

In *In re Elmendorf,* 345 B.R. 486 (Bankr. S.D.N.Y. 2006), the court concluded that dismissal for cause pursuant to §707(a) is not always the appropriate disposition of a petition that has been filed by a debtor ineligible for bankruptcy relief pursuant to §109(h), and that the "court may choose to strike or dismiss a petition in view of the particular circumstances *sub judice* in the exercise of its equitable powers pursuant to §105(a) to carry out Congressional intent that individuals receive credit counseling before filing for bankruptcy relief." In *In re Thompson,* 344 B.R. 899 (Bankr. S.D. Ind. 2006), *vacated as moot,* 249 Fed. Appx. 475 (7th Cir. 2007), the court held that when a putative debtor who filed a bankruptcy petition is ineligible because he did not comply with

---

83   11 U.S.C. §362(c)(3)(A).

§109(h)'s credit counseling requirement, the proper remedy is to strike the petition, not to dismiss the case. Interestingly, the court further found that the filing of a petition by an ineligible debtor triggers the automatic stay, even though no "case" has been commenced. The opinion was subsequently vacated as moot on other grounds.

In *In re Rios,* 336 B.R. 177 (Bankr. S.D.N.Y. 2005), the court found that the putative debtor, who neither sought prepetition credit counseling nor made the appropriate certification to the court evidencing eligibility for an exemption from the credit-counseling requirement, never properly commenced a case and, thus, the petition would be stricken, as opposed to dismissed. Finally, in a perplexing case from a proceduralist perspective, in *Adams v. Finlay,* 2006 WL 3240522 (S.D.N.Y. Nov. 03, 2006), the district court found that the bankruptcy judge acted within her judicial power when striking a petition where the debtor failed to obtain credit counseling prior to filing. "Failure to receive counseling in compliance with the statute is not jurisdictional, rather it goes to whether the petition states a claim upon which relief can be granted." Therefore, according to the court, striking the petition rather than dismissal was a proper remedy.

2. Dismiss

In *In re Mason,* 2007 WL 433077 (E.D. Ky. Feb. 5, 2007), the district court overturned the bankruptcy court's decision to strike the petition rather than dismiss the case. The district court found that the bankruptcy court had exceeded its jurisdiction under §105. The district court found that "there is no support for the remedy of striking a debtor's petition in the Bankruptcy Code. On the other hand, the dismissal remedy is explicitly set forth in section 707 and is not limited to the conditions enumerated in that section." *Id.* at *3. Likewise, in *In re Dyer,* 381 B.R. 200 (Bankr. W.D.N.C. 2007), the court held that the petition filed by a debtor who, due to lack of prepetition credit counseling, is not eligible to be bankruptcy debtor, is not a legal nullity that has to be stricken, but rather is subject to being dismissed. Additionally, in *In re Enloe,* 373 B.R. 123 (Bankr. D. Colo. 2007), the court observed that the credit counseling requirement imposed as a prerequisite to an individual's being eligible for bankruptcy relief is not jurisdictional, and until the bankruptcy court determines debtor's eligibility, the bankruptcy case actually exists, that cannot thereafter be deemed a nullity simply by striking the case. In *In re Falcone,* 370 B.R. 462 (Bankr. D. Mass. 2007), the court held that the appropriate remedy for failing to comply with §109(h) was an order dismissing, rather than striking as *void ab initio,* the debtor's chapter 13 case. *See also In re Swiatkowski,* 356 B.R. 581 (Bankr. E.D.N.Y. 2006) ("The law is clear that, with limited exceptions, a Debtor must obtain credit counseling prior to filing in order to be eligible to file a petition in bankruptcy." Additionally, "the Court declines to follow that line of cases which 'strike' rather than dismiss petitions."); *In re Wilson,* 346 B.R. 59 (Bankr. N.D.N.Y. 2006) (appropriate disposition, upon determination by bankruptcy court that debtors had not satisfied prepetition credit counseling requirement and were not entitled to extension based on exigent circumstances, was to dismiss, not strike, bankruptcy case); *In re Tomco,* 339 B.R. 145 (Bankr. W.D. Pa. 2006) ("cause" for dismissal of bankruptcy case is not limited to enumerated statutory list(s); debtor's ineligibility for bankruptcy relief constitutes one "cause" for dismissal of case; further, debtor was ineligible to be debtor, so proper remedy was dismissal, as opposed to striking petition as *void ab initio*); *In re Wallace,* 338 B.R. 399 (Bankr. E.D. Ark. 2006) (chapter 13 debtor's failure to seek or obtain credit counseling prior to filing her bankruptcy petition, and failure to provide any certificate of exigent circumstances, rendered her ineligible for bankruptcy relief and necessitated dismissal of petition); *In re Dillard,* 2006 WL 3658485 (Bankr. M.D. Ga. Dec. 11, 2006) (appropriate method for dealing with case of ineligible debtor is dismissal of case because "the eligibility question is not jurisdictional and does not prevent an ineligible debtor from commencing a case and having that case dismissed"); *In re Cannon,* 376 B.R. 847 (Bankr. M.D. Tenn. 2006) (dismissal of chapter 13 case, as opposed to striking of bankruptcy petition, was appropriate outcome where individuals were ineligible to be debtors due to their failure to obtain requisite prepetition credit counseling). See also the discussion above in III.C.1.a.

E. Exemptions and Extensions

The Bankruptcy Code contains several exemptions from the requirement under §109(h) that a debtor obtain credit counseling before he may file a petition. Each of the following sections addresses a particular exemption or extension.

1. U.S. Trustee Certification of Insufficient Providers— §109(h)(2)

Section 109(h)(2) exempts certain debtors from the credit counseling requirement who do not have available to them credit counseling services in their district as certified by the U.S. Trustee. The impetus behind the exemption is to recognize that in some areas of the country, potential debtors simply may not have access to certified counseling providers. In *In re Hubbard,* 333 B.R. 377 (Bankr. S.D. Tex. 2005), the court held that where the U.S. Trustee presented sufficient evidence that credit counseling services were available to the debtors and where the majority of other debtors in the same district complied with the credit counseling requirement, there was insufficient evidence for the debtors to find relief under §109(h)(2). Thus, the debtors must comply with the prepetition counseling requirements under §109(h). In contrast, in *In re Hubbard,* 332 B.R 285 (Bankr. S.D. Tex. 2005), the court found that §109(h)(2) excused the debtors from the credit counseling requirement where the U.S. Trustee determined that approved agencies were not reasonably able to provide such services in the given district. However, the debtor could not seek relief under this provision because the Southern District of Texas was not so classified.

In *In re McBride,* 354 B.R. 95 (Bankr. D. S.C. 2006), the court observed that the U.S. Trustees for Regions 4 and 21, respectively, have not determined that the approved credit counseling providers for South Carolina and the federal judicial districts of Georgia are not reasonably able to provide adequate services to debtors. Thus, according to the court, §109(h)(2) does not afford the debtor an exemption. Moreover, in *In re Mingueta,* 338 B.R. 833 (Bankr. C.D. Cal. 2006), the court acknowledged that the U.S. Trustee has not found that there are insufficient accredited credit counselors in the Central District of California. Thus, the credit counseling requirement could not be waived pursuant to §109(h)(2).

In the wake of Hurricane Katrina, the U.S. Trustee issued waivers for four affected districts. However, as of August 2008, all of the waivers had been lifted with the exception of the area surrounding New Orleans (Eastern District of Louisiana).

2. Exigent Circumstances—§109(h)(3)

Section 109(h)(3) grants an exemption from the credit counseling requirement in certain exigent circumstances. Cases suggest this exemption should be strictly construed.

a. What Type of Certification of Exigent Circumstances Is Required?

i. Verified

In *In re Hubbard,* 333 B.R. 377 (Bankr. S.D. Tex. 2005), the court found that where the debtors did not file an appropriate verified statement of exigent circumstances pursuant to §109(h)(3), but later filed a verified statement that they received the counseling post-petition, the debtors were still ineligible to be debtors on their petition date. Further, the court reaffirmed its prior finding in the matter that applications and unsworn statements did not meet the requirements for this provision. *See In re Hubbard,* 333 B.R. 373 (Bankr. S.D. Tex. 2005) (applications for consideration of exigent circumstances under §109(h)(3) are not sufficient to meet the requirements for "certificate;" until such certifications were filed, court refused to consider exigency of circumstances.). *See also In re Hubbard,* 332 B.R 285 (Bankr. S.D. Tex. 2005) (extension cannot be granted under plain meaning of §109(h)(3) without "affidavit, declaration or other certification as to its accuracy;" simple unverified motion would not suffice).

In *In re Wilson,* 346 B.R. 59 (Bankr. N.D.N.Y. 2006), the bankruptcy court held that the certification of exigent circumstances must be the certification of debtors, not their counsel. In other words, the facts relied upon must be attested to by those with actual knowledge of the facts and circumstances. In *In re Cobb,* 343 B.R. 204 (Bankr. E.D. Ark.

2006), the court elaborated further on the question of what information is necessary to support an assertion that exigent circumstances exist in order to exempt a debtor from credit counseling before filing a bankruptcy petition. According to the court, the "certification" that a debtor must submit in order to obtain a temporary waiver of the credit counseling requirement must contain facts that are sworn to under oath. In that case, the typed statement submitted by the *pro se* chapter 13 debtors, which was not sworn to under penalty of perjury, did not constitute a "certification" as required for debtors to obtain a temporary waiver of the credit counseling requirement, even though the document was signed by each and dated.

In *In re Mingueta,* 338 B.R. 833 (Bankr. C.D. Cal. 2006), the court discusses what is necessary to support a finding that exigent circumstances exist. Thus, to obtain a waiver of the credit counseling requirement, a putative debtor must meet all the requirements of §109(h)(3). An unsubstantiated request that does not specify the circumstances or the steps taken to attempt to obtain such counseling is insufficient. Moreover, in *In re DiPinto,* 336 B.R. 693 (Bankr. E.D. Pa. 2006), the court held that: (1) a statement signed by counsel was insufficient to meet the certification requirement; (2) a token effort at obtaining credit counseling at 5:00 p.m. on the eve of the filing was insufficient; and (3) imminent foreclosure on the day of the filing was not exigent where the putative debtor did not sufficiently explain why he delayed seeking assistance. Thus, the court dismissed the case. Likewise, in *In re Rodriguez,* 336 B.R. 462 (Bankr. D. Idaho 2005), the debtor sought an exemption from the credit counseling requirement. The court determined that the certification must be personally verified by the debtors and in a form consistent with the federal statute governing declarations, verifications and certificates submitted under penalty of perjury. The certification must also contain all relevant facts that the debtors are urging the court to consider. In the end, the court is looking for facts sufficient to constitute exigent circumstances that must distinguish the debtor from those putative debtors generally expected to comply with the counseling requirement. Finally, in *In re LaPorta,* 332 B.R. 879 (Bankr. D. Minn. 2005), the court held that a debtor's unsworn statement that she did an Internet search and could not find an accredited agency that she could afford to reach for such services, particularly where she made no attempt to actually contact such services, was insufficient to meet the criteria for exigent circumstances under §109(h)(3).

ii. Unverified

Other courts have rejected the requirement that the certification of exigent circumstances must be verified or sworn. For example, in *In re Henderson,* 339 B.R. 34 (Bankr. E.D.N.Y. 2006), the court held that the certification seeking a temporary exemption from the credit counseling requirement need not be signed under penalty of perjury. Nonetheless, the court found that the debtor's statement was insufficient where it did not distinguish her from other debtors expected to meet the credit counseling requirement. In *In re Talib,* 335 B.R. 417 (Bankr. W.D. Mo. 2005), although the court found that the debtor's unsworn statement was sufficient under the provisions of §109(h)(3), the court further found that the other conditions of the provision were not met where the debtor failed to request credit counseling prior to filing her petition. Thus, the case was dismissed due to lack of eligibility.

b. Are the Requirements for Exigency Met?

i. Requirements Not Met

Even assuming that the debtor has employed the specific form of certification to support a claim of exigent circumstances, the debtor must allege sufficient facts and circumstances that will distinguish him or her from other putative debtors expected to conform. Thus, in *In re Hedquist,* 342 B.R. 295 (B.A.P. 8th Cir. 2006), the court affirmed a bankruptcy court's decision that the debtors' delay in waiting to file a bankruptcy petition until the eve of the mortgage foreclosure sale, despite the fact that the debtors had ample notice thereof, did not constitute "exigent circumstances" such as might permit the temporary waiver of the prepetition credit counseling requirement. Further, in *In re Dixon,* 338 B.R. 383 (B.A.P. 8th Cir. 2006), the court held that a bankruptcy court did not abuse its discretion when determining that the threatened loss of a chapter 13 debtor's home at a foreclosure sale scheduled to occur one day after the bankruptcy petition was filed did not rise to the level of exigent circumstances that merited a waiver of the prepetition credit counseling requirement. The court found that the debtor had ample advance notice of the foreclosure sale, but waited until one day prior thereto to contact an attorney. According to the court, the requirement that the debtor demonstrate exigent circumstances meriting a waiver of the credit counseling requirement has at least two substantive components. First, as the court noted, there must be exigent circumstances presented. Second, as the court further observed, those circumstances must merit a waiver.

In *In re Hoshan,* 2008 WL 81994 (E.D. Pa. Jan. 7, 2008), the court initially found that the credit counseling requirement was not jurisdictional. Noting that the debtor did not get credit counseling until after she had filed her petition, the court noted that she actually had not sought an exigent circumstances waiver. Recognizing that her family situation was difficult, the court found that such difficulty did not rise to the level of those cases in which courts avoid manifest injustice by waiving the credit counseling requirement.

In *In re Wilson,* 346 B.R. 59 (Bankr. N.D.N.Y. 2006), the bankruptcy court held that: (1) to obtain an extension of time to obtain credit counseling based on exigent circumstances, the debtors must have requested such counseling prepetition; (2) the certification of exigent circumstances must be the certification of debtors, not their counsel; and (3) the appropriate disposition, upon determination by the bankruptcy court that the debtors had not satisfied the prepetition credit counseling requirement and were not entitled to an extension based on exigent circumstances, was to dismiss, not strike, the bankruptcy case. The court observed that both the term "waiver" and "exemption" were misnomers since what the statute sought to provide the debtor with was an "extension" of time to comply with the credit counseling requirement.

Furthermore, in *In re Childs,* 335 B.R. 623 (Bankr. D. Md. 2005), several consolidated cases, the consensus of the bankruptcy court judges was that: (1) debtors demonstrated "exigent circumstances" by asserting the imminent sale of their property at foreclosure and/or their imminent eviction from their residences; (2) debtors' certification of post-petition credit counseling was insufficient to grant a waiver of credit counseling; (3) certifications that did not mention any attempt by debtors to obtain credit counseling or that stated that debtors were unable to obtain credit counseling were insufficient to grant a waiver of credit counseling; and (4) debtors' failure to file satisfactory certifications for a waiver of credit counseling and/or proper certificates of credit counseling required dismissal of their cases.

In *Clippard v. Bass,* 365 B.R. 131 (W.D. Tenn. 2007), the district court held that the request filed by a *pro se* chapter 7 debtor for temporary deferral of the credit counseling requirement could not be granted on an "exigent circumstances" theory. In this case, the debtor, while certifying that credit counseling was offered in that district only once per month, and that the next session would occur more than one week later, failed to explain why she had to file her petition immediately and why she could not have waited until after attending this monthly session in order to file her petition. Moreover, the debtor, in failing to specify when she had first requested credit counseling, did not provide sufficient information to permit the court to determine that counseling could not have been obtained within five days of the debtor's request. Likewise, in *In re Shea,* 2008 WL 80245 (Bankr. E.D. Va. Jan. 7, 2008), the court held that absent a request for services and the agency's inability to provide counseling within the five-day period, the court has no power to grant a request for waiver, no matter how compelling the circumstances.

In In re Afolabi, 343 B.R. 195 (Bankr. S.D. Ind. 2006), the court held that the proper focus under the exigent circumstances extension was not on the circumstances that hastened or precipitated the bankruptcy filing: rather, proper focus centered on whether those circumstances or any others prevented the debtor from being able to obtain credit counseling prior to the filing for bankruptcy. "As several other courts have pointed out, §109(h)'s requirements may lead to harsh and arguably inequitable results. However, enforcement of §109(h) is mandatory. The Court has no discretion but to dismiss a case when the debtor fails to file a certification in compliance with its provisions."

Various courts have also found a lack of exigent circumstances in a wide variety of fact patterns:

FORECLOSURE SALES

In re Postlethwait, 353 B.R. 428 (Bankr. W.D. Pa. 2006) (certification of exigent circumstances filed by chapter 13 debtor requesting temporary waiver of credit counseling requirement, in reciting only that debtor had contacted two agencies in unsuccessful attempt to obtain required counseling roughly 40 minutes before her petition was filed and six days prior to the creditor's sale that was alleged to be exigent circumstance that necessitated prompt filing of petition, did not sufficiently allege "inability" on debtor's part to obtain required counseling); *In re Carr,* 344 B.R. 774 (Bankr. N.D. W.Va. 2006) (chapter 13 debtor was not entitled to temporary waiver based on exigent circumstances even assuming he could show exigent circumstances based on impending mortgage foreclosure sale where debtor did not request credit counseling services from approved nonprofit budget and credit counseling agency before filing his petition, and thus could not show that he had requested, but been unable, to obtain such services); *In re Toccaline,* 2006 WL 2081517 (Bankr. D. Conn. July 17, 2006) (court found that while impending foreclosure in wake of failed attempts at refinancing was "exigent circumstance," inability to get counseling due to inability to pay $50 fee within five-day period was not sufficient to meet requirements of §109(h)(3)(A)(ii)).

INMATES

In re Rendler, 368 B.R. 1 (Bankr. D. Minn. 2007) (case had to be dismissed on eligibility grounds given that debtor-inmate had not requested temporary waiver of credit counseling requirement based on exigent circumstances and would not have benefited therefrom in any event given his ongoing inability to obtain such counseling and his inability to obtain counseling was not result of incapacity, disability or service in military combat zone, as those terms were narrowly defined in Code provision permitting, in very limited circumstances, permanent waiver of credit counseling requirement); *In re Latovljevic,* 343 B.R. 817 (Bankr. N.D. W.Va. 2006) (chapter 13 debtor who, though incarcerated at federal correctional institution, was not incapacitated or disabled in any way, and who made no attempt to avail himself of opportunities available to him to obtain credit counseling prepetition by telephone, was not entitled to temporary waiver or exemption from credit counseling requirement).

FAILURE TO SEEK COUNSELING IN TIME

In re Randolph, 342 B.R. 633 (Bankr. M.D. Fla. 2005) (exigent circumstances extension does not extend to debtor who "simply fails to prioritize the counseling requirement"); *In re Carey,* 341 B.R. 798 (Bankr. M.D. Fla. 2006) (debtors did not meet requirements of §109(h) where they failed to contact credit counseling agency until 30 minutes after they filed their petition and did not receive the counseling until post-petition.); *In re Tomco,* 339 B.R. 145 (Bankr. W.D. Pa. 2006) (where individual seeking chapter 13 relief acknowledged that she did not contact approved credit counseling agency before she filed her bankruptcy petition, so that her certificate of exigent circumstances was deficient and she was ineligible to be debtor, proper remedy was for bankruptcy court to dismiss); *In re Valdez,* 335 B.R. 801 (Bankr. S.D. Fla. 2005) (ignorance of requirement for credit counseling until time in which it was too late to obtain such counseling was not sufficient to be exigent circumstance); *In re Talib,* 335 B.R. 424 (Bankr. W.D. Mo. 2005) (on motion for rehearing of dismissal of debtor's case, court determined that while requiring prospective debtors to certify that credit counseling could not have been obtained within five days in order to obtain a temporary waiver may result in harsh rulings, such requirement did not rise to level of absurdity so as to allow bankruptcy court to interpret statute other than via its plain meaning); *In re Talib,* 335 B.R. 417 (Bankr. W.D. Mo. 2005) (while court found debtor's unsworn statement to be sufficient under provisions of §109(h)(3), the court found that other conditions of provision were not met where debtor failed to request credit counseling prior to filing her petition); *In re Davenport,* 335 B.R. 218 (Bankr. M.D. Fla. 2005) (while court found that debtor had shown exigent circumstances, relief from requirements of §109(h) was not available because she failed to request credit counseling before filing; fact that debtor received such counseling post-petition did not cure the error); *In re LaPorta,* 332 B.R. 879 (Bankr. D. Minn. 2005) (debtor's unsworn statements that she did Internet search and could not find accredited agency that she could afford to reach for such services, particularly where she did not make any attempts to actually contact such services, were insufficient to meet the criteria for exigent circumstances under §109(h)(3)); *In re Gee,* 332 B.R. 602 (Bankr. W.D. Mo. 2005) ("The Debtor can be eligible for a waiver under §109(h)(3) only if each of the following three requirements is met: (1) the certification describes exigent circumstances that merit a waiver; (2) it states that the debtor requested credit counseling services from an approved agency, but was unable to obtain the services during the five-day period beginning on the date on which the debtor made the request; and (3) the certification is satisfactory to the Court. These requirements are stated in the conjunctive, meaning that each of the three requirements must be met.").

FAILURE TO DISTINGUISH FROM OTHER DEBTORS

In re Henderson, 339 B.R. 34 (Bankr. E.D.N.Y. 2006) (while finding that certification seeking temporary exemption from credit counseling requirement need not be signed under penalty of perjury, court nonetheless found that debtor's statement was insufficient where it did not distinguish her from other debtors expected to meet credit counseling requirement); *In re DiPinto,* 336 B.R. 693 (Bankr. E.D. Pa. 2006) (court held that statement signed by counsel was insufficient to meet certification requirement; token effort at obtaining credit counseling at 5:00 p.m. on eve of filing was insufficient; imminent foreclosure on day of filing was not exigent where putative debtor did not sufficiently explain why he delayed in seeking assistance); *In re Rodriguez,* 336 B.R. 462 (Bankr. D. Idaho 2005) (certification must be document in which debtors personally verify, in form consistent with federal statute governing declarations, verifications and certificates submitted under penalty of perjury, facts that they wish court to consider; exigent circumstances that are alleged must distinguish debtor from those generally expected to comply with requirement).

FACTS NOT SUFFICIENTLY SET OUT IN STATEMENT

In re Piontek, 346 B.R. 126 (Bankr. W.D. Pa. 2006) (bankruptcy court held that: (1) debtor who lacks sufficient resources to pay for credit counseling may, under right circumstances, have *de facto* "inability" to obtain pre-bankruptcy credit counseling, and this "inability" to pay for credit counseling may be "satisfactory" reason for court to grant temporary waiver of the credit counseling requirement; but (2) debtors' alleged lack of financial resources to pay, prepetition, two $50 fees that allegedly would have been required for both debtors to obtain prepetition credit counseling was not sufficiently established by evidence in record); *In re Anderson*, 2006 WL 314539 (Bankr. N.D. Iowa, Feb. 6, 2006) (failure to show facts and circumstances surrounding garnishment of wages and timing of payment of such wages was insufficient to show exigency; without specifying when wages are to be paid and why filing was necessary before counseling could be obtained, there was not showing of exigency; further, where co-debtor did not sign statement regarding exigency, his case was dismissed outright).

ii. Requirements Met

Several courts have been more receptive to arguments advanced by debtors in these circumstances. For example, in *In re Henderson*, 364 B.R. 906 (Bankr. N.D. Tex. 2007), the court was persuaded that the foreclosure on a family home is a circumstance requiring immediate aid or action, particularly in the State of Texas, where nonjudicial foreclosure sales are permitted on very short notice to a borrower. Thus, a home foreclosure itself may satisfy the "exigent circumstance" element of a debtor's request for extension of time to complete credit counseling. Further, according to the court, the statute was ambiguous, given that, due to Congress' use of the word "during," the statute could be interpreted to apply to the debtor who requested counseling services but was not able to obtain those services through duration of the five-day period beginning on the date which the request was made, or to the debtor who requested services but was unable to obtain them at a point during the course or in the five-day period beginning on the date on which request was made.

In *In re Giambrone*, 365 B.R. 386 (Bankr. W.D.N.Y. 2007), the court found that where the chapter 13 debtors requested credit counseling services on the day prior to their bankruptcy filing, which also was the day prior to the scheduled foreclosure sale of their real property, were unable to obtain those services before bankruptcy, and ultimately completed credit counseling on the fifth day after their request, the bankruptcy court could grant an extension of time to complete credit counseling, even though credit counseling was available within five days, but not before the exigent event. The court noted that when exigent circumstances require bankruptcy protection in fewer than five days, the window for completion of the counseling must collapse into the amount of time that is available. Thus, the test was not whether the agency can provide a counseling session within five days, but whether, in the context of their circumstances, the debtors can complete within five days the counseling that must otherwise occur prior to that exigent moment when a bankruptcy filing is necessary. Moreover, the court in *In re Romero,* 349 B.R. 616 (Bankr. N.D. Cal. 2006), found that the would-be chapter 7 debtors who, three days before filing for bankruptcy relief, had requested credit counseling from an approved agency but been unable to obtain it within the requisite five-day period specified by statute, and who had the need to file for bankruptcy in order to prevent garnishment of debtor-husband's wages, sufficiently established requisite "exigent circumstances" and were entitled to a temporary waiver of the credit counseling requirement.

There do exist, however, certain limits to the logic. For example, in *In re Star,* 341 B.R. 830 (Bankr. E.D. Va. 2006), the court found that the debtor's incarceration was not the sort of incapacitation or disability that would exempt the debtor from credit counseling pursuant to §109(h)(4). However, the court did find that the incarceration was sufficient to meet the exigent circumstances temporary exemption.

3. Disability, Incapacity and the Military—§109(h)(4)

Section 109(h)(4) exempts certain debtors from the credit counseling requirement based on status such as disability, incapacity and military.

a. Incarcerated Debtors

Incarcerated debtors pose a difficult question as to whether their status should constitute grounds to support a finding of exigent circumstances as discussed above. Courts have disagreed over whether such status renders a debtor disabled for purposes of obtaining credit counseling.

i. Not Disabled or Incapacitated

In *In re Rendler,* 368 B.R. 1 (Bankr. D. Minn. 2007), the court held that the bankruptcy case had to be dismissed on eligibility grounds given that the incarcerated debtor had not requested a temporary waiver of the credit-counseling requirement based on exigent circumstances. Moreover, the court observed that even if the debtor had requested a temporary waiver based on exigent circumstances, he would not have benefited therefrom in any event given his ongoing inability to obtain such counseling because of his incarceration. Following the line of thought embraced by cases in this camp, the court stated that the debtor's inability to obtain counseling was not a result of incapacity, disability or service in a military combat zone, as those terms were narrowly defined in §109(h), a provision permitting, in very limited circumstances, a permanent waiver of the credit-counseling requirement.

In *In re McBride,* 354 B.R. 95 (Bankr. D. S.C. 2006), the debtor's incarceration did not render him exempt from the credit-counseling requirement. The court found that incarceration does not constitute a type of incapacity or disability. Therefore, the incarcerated debtor's failure to obtain credit counseling constituted cause to dismiss the case. Moreover, in *In re Latovljevic,* 343 B.R. 817 (Bankr. N.D. W.Va. 2006), the court held that a chapter 13 debtor who, though incarcerated at a federal correctional institution, was not incapacitated or disabled in any way. He made no attempt to avail himself of opportunities available to him to obtain credit counseling prepetition by telephone and was not entitled to a temporary waiver or exemption from the credit-counseling requirement. Based on these findings, the court ruled that the chapter 13 case had to be dismissed on the ground that he was not eligible for such relief because of his failure to comply with §109(h). Lastly, in *In re Star,* 341 B.R. 830 (Bankr. E.D. Va. 2006), the court held that the debtor's incarceration was not the sort of incapacitation or disability that would permanently exempt the debtor from credit counseling pursuant to §109(h)(4). However, the court did find that the incarceration was sufficient to meet the exigent circumstances temporary exemption.

ii. Disabled or Incapacitated

In *In re Gates*, 2007 WL 4365474 (Bankr. E.D. Cal. Dec. 12, 2007), the court articulated an approach that would result in a finding that the incarcerated debtor was disabled within the meaning of §109(h)(4). The court specifically found:

> The debtor is "disabled" within the meaning ascribed in Section 109(h)(4)... He is therefore unable to physically attend a personal financial management course. He also lacks access to the Internet and due to constraints placed by the California Department of Corrections, debtor cannot contact debtor education agencies by phone.

Moreover, *In re Vollmer*, 361 B.R. 811 (Bankr. E.D. Va. 2007), the court held that an incarcerated chapter 7 debtor, who had no telephone or computer access other than the ability to make collect calls, was unable to participate in required credit-counseling and financial-management courses. Therefore, according to the court, a permanent waiver of those requirements was warranted, even though debtor's imprisonment, standing alone, was not a "disability" sufficient to merit the waiver of the counseling requirement.

b. Dead Debtors

The death of a debtor poses thorny issues under BAPCPA. One of these issues is whether death legally (as opposed to practically) excuses any prepetition counseling or pre-discharge educational requirement. In *In re Trembulak*, 2007 WL 420188 (Bankr. D. N.J. 2007), the court held that the debtor, who died after filing a chapter 7 petition, was legally exempted from BAPCPA's credit-counseling requirements, and thus could not be denied a discharge on that basis alone.

c. Other Disabilities and Incapacities

Courts have struggled with the questions of whether other mental or physical conditions may constitute a legal excuse from the counseling requirements. For example, in *In re Jarrell*, 364 B.R. 899 (Bankr. N.D. Tex. 2007), the court found that a chapter 7 debtor, who had a mental illness, had the requisite incapacity to justify a waiver of the §109(h) prepetition credit-counseling requirement. The court supported its findings based on the debtor's psychologist, who testified that while the debtor could identify specific assets or debts, he did not understand, and could not reasonably be expected to make decisions that required him to understand, the relationship between the two. In *In re Howard,* 359 B.R. 589 (Bankr. E.D.N.C. 2007), the court held that a chapter 13 debtor suffered from a physical disability and, thus, was exempt from the prepetition credit-counseling requirement. The court found that the debtor was required to travel to obtain dialysis treatments and had been hospitalized, suffered cardiac arrest and placed on life support for approximately 14 days. The court further found that since his release from the hospital, the debtor had suffered from short-term memory loss, hearing loss and limited mobility.

In *In re Hall,* 347 B.R. 532 (Bankr. N.D. W.Va. 2006), the court found that a chapter 7 debtor was entitled to a disability waiver of the postpetition/predischarge instructional course concerning personal financial management. The court further found that although the debtor was capable of some mobility, as he was able to visit his attorney's office, the courtroom and the location of his prepetition credit counseling, the debtor demonstrated a severe physical impairment. Facts that supported this finding included that the debtor was 81 years old, hearing-impaired, limited to a scooter for mobility and suffered from serious health issues, including prostate cancer. The court was also impressed by the fact that the debtor made a reasonable effort to complete the instructional course concerning personal financial management but was unable to do because of his limited mental capacity, hearing impairment and other physical impairments. Therefore, the court concluded that the course would be of no benefit to the debtor in avoiding future financial distress.

In another case of interest, the court in *In re Tulper,* 345 B.R. 322 (Bankr. D. Colo. 2006), held that the chapter 13 debtors were entitled to a permanent "disability" exemption from the credit-counseling requirement where it was apparent that debtors were severely physically impaired. In this case, the court found that the debtor-wife was not very ambulatory because she was tethered to a breathing apparatus and was wheelchair-bound. The court further found that the debtor-husband was virtually deaf and his hands and feet were disabled. Again, the court was impressed that the debtors had undertaken reasonable efforts to address credit counseling by conferring with an accountant and an attorney, and that the debtors, though competent and lucid, were unable to sufficiently comprehend information necessary to formulate a budget and analyze finances because of their physical condition. Therefore, according to the court, the debtors were unable to participate in a meaningful way in any credit counseling.

Language may also pose an obstacle to obtaining credit counseling. In *In re Petit-Louis*, 344 B.R. 696 (Bankr. S.D. Fla. 2006), the court held that the debtor was entitled to a waiver of the credit-counseling requirement based on the fact that when the petition was filed, there were no approved counseling agencies in the district that offered the credit counseling in Creole. The court further held that where the debtor, for whom the filing fee had been waived, had only limited English and the U.S. Trustee could not provide either a translator or Creole-speaking counselors, the counseling would be of little benefit. Thus, according to the court, the counseling requirement was waived. Interestingly, the court's holding was under §109(h)(2), not 109(h)(4); the court found that it had the authority to review the U.S. Trustee's decision that approved counselors in the district were reasonably able to provide credit counseling to debtors in the district.

F. A Sword or a Shield? Using the Failure to Get Credit Counseling to Dismiss Your Own Case

As experienced bankruptcy practitioners, it should not surprise us that certain debtors would seek to use the consequences of failing to meet the pre-filing credit-counseling requirements as a means to cause the premature termination of their cases when advantageous to do so. For example, in *In re Mendez*, 367 B.R. 109 (B.A.P. 9th Cir. 2007), the court confronted that precise situation. In that case, the court found that the debtor waived strict compliance with the prebankruptcy credit-counseling requirements, and so was not entitled to use her noncompliance offensively as a basis for dismissal. Furthermore, in *In re Warren*, 378 B.R. 640 (N.D. Cal. 2007), the district court held that the bankruptcy court did not err in its determination that judicial *estoppel* could act to prevent the debtor from dismissing his own case for failure to obtain the required credit counseling. In *In re Lilliefors,* 379 B.R. 608 (Bankr. E.D. Va. 2007), the court also employed the doctrine of judicial *estoppel* to prevent a debtor from using the credit-counseling requirement as a sword. The court held:

> The debtor is judicially estopped from benefiting by obtaining dismissal of his case for non-compliance with §109(h)(1). The debtor's certification under penalty of perjury that he completed credit counseling within 180 days before filing his bankruptcy petition, a requirement to commence his case, is adequate, unless challenged, to satisfy the credit-counseling requirement. He may not now disavow that statement because creditors will be prejudiced if the case is dismissed... Because the debtor is judicially estopped from denying that he completed the requisite credit counseling, it is not necessary that a credit counseling certificate be filed.

In *In re Timmerman,* 379 B.R. 838 (Bankr. N.D. Iowa 2007), the court stated that it had the discretion to refrain from ordering a dismissal where the debtors sought to dismiss for their own failure to comply with the pre-filing counseling requirements. Finally, in *In re Parker,* 351 B.R. 790 (Bankr. N.D. Ga. 2006), the court held that the debtor who, after becoming aware that the entity from which he obtained credit counseling prepetition was not an approved credit counseling agency, waived his right to rely on the ineligibility provisions as a basis for the voluntary dismissal of his case, particularly where there existed an unexplained delay in seeking such relief.[84]

G. Reopening Cases for Debtor Education – A Second Educational Requirement

In several cases, courts have confronted attempts by debtors who insist that compliance with one educational requirement imposed by BAPCPA should satisfy any other educational requirement. In particular, debtors have sought to argue that compliance with the

---

84   See also *In re Racette,* 343 B.R. 200 (Bankr. E.D. Wis. 2006) (court held that prior chapter 13 case filed by debtors who, contrary to certain representations made on face of their prior petition, had not in fact received pre-petition credit counseling and were, therefore, not eligible to be bankruptcy debtors was not a mere nullity; thus, court could strike petition and not treat as prior case, for purpose of deciding what type of stay arose in second chapter 13 case which debtors filed same date that prior case was dismissed; prior case, which was administered for almost 90 days, and in which trustee was appointed, meeting of creditors was held, order was entered requiring debtors to begin making plan payments and motion for relief from stay was filed, was treated as a case and not as mere nullity by all parties in interest).

pre-filing credit-counseling requirement should satisfy any need to satisfy any predischarge educational requirement. However, there are two distinct educational requirements—one prepetition and one predischarge. Of course, that raises the question of what happens when a debtor fails to satisfy the second requirement. For example, in *In re Lauro,* 2007 WL 4180683 (W.D. Pa. Nov. 20, 2007), a case in which the debtors were not advised by their counsel to file their postpetition financial management course certificate even though they completed the course within the time limit, the court held that "despite their failure to comply with the 45-day time limit specified by Interim Bankruptcy Rule 1007(c), the [Debtors] are entitled under *Pioneer* to an equitable inquiry regarding the issue raised with respect to excusable neglect…This court finds that the [Debtors] meet their burden of showing excusable neglect and holds as a matter of equity that their bankruptcy case will be reopened." *Id.* at *8. In *In re Knight,* 349 B.R. 681 (Bankr. D. Idaho 2006), the debtor urged the reopening of his case to allow him to file the required certification of completion of the financial management course and obtain a discharge. According to the court, this showing provided sufficient cause to reopen the case since doing so would be, in the Code's language, "to accord relief to the debtor." 349 B.R. at 685. However, the court observed that a waiver of the reopening fee need not be routinely or automatically granted; according to the court, this is a matter of discretion and may be waived if "appropriate circumstances" have been shown. *Id.* at 687.

In *In re Hassett,* 341 B.R. 832 (Bankr. E.D. Va. 2006), the court observed that, in light of the newness of BAPCPA, the debtor's violation by failing to file her certification that showed that she had completed a course in personal financial management within 45 days of first date set for the meeting of creditors constituted cause for the bankruptcy court to reopen her chapter 7 case, which was closed without granting the debtor a discharge. The reopening of the case in order to give the debtor an opportunity to file and properly notice the required motion to extend the time to file her certificate of financial management would allow her to receive her discharge upon a proper showing.

IV.

Application of §707(b) to Converted Cases

BAPCPA dramatically changed several aspects of individual consumer bankruptcy law and, for the first time, imposed what is commonly known as a "means test" to determine individual consumer debtor eligibility for relief under chapter 7 of the Bankruptcy Code. BAPCPA generally became effective as to cases filed on or after Oct. 17, 2005.

The means test is found in §707(b) of the Bankruptcy Code.[85] That section was amended to provide for dismissal of chapter 7 cases, or conversion to chapter 13 (with the debtor's consent), upon a finding of abuse of the bankruptcy process by an individual debtor with primarily consumer debts. There are two ways to find abuse. First, abuse may be found through an unrebutted presumption of abuse, arising under a new means test. Second, abuse may be found on general grounds, including bad faith and/or the totality of the circumstances, determined after notice and hearing.

The presumption of abuse, set out in §707(b)(2), is triggered by a means test designed to determine the extent of a debtor's ability to repay general unsecured claims. The means test has three elements: (1)

---

85   For an excellent discussion of the means test and some of the present problems in its application, see Eugene R. Wedoff, Major Consumer Bankruptcy Effects of BAPCPA, 2007 Illinois L. Rev. 31. Further, the first two webinars in the ABI's Consumer Bankruptcy in Practice series addressed the means test in detail and may be purchased at abiworld.org.

a definition of "current monthly income," measuring the total income a debtor is presumed to have available; (2) a list of allowed deductions from current monthly income, for purposes of support and repayment of higher priority debt; and (3) a defined "threshold of abuse" at which the income remaining after the allowed deductions would result in a presumption of abuse.[86] Practice under the Bankruptcy Code has established that the application of the means test is a complex process and has increased the costs of chapter 7 bankruptcy representation.

The other basis for a finding of abuse, applicable under §707(b)(3) where the presumption does not apply or has been rebutted, is that the debtor filed the petition in bad faith, or that the totality of the debtor's financial circumstances indicates abuse. The U.S. Trustee, bankruptcy administrator or judge can assert this basis for finding abuse in any case; creditors and case trustees are limited to asserting it in cases where the debtor's income is above the defined state median. The totality-of-circumstances test is a fact-specific inquiry. Under this approach, a bankruptcy court holds an evidentiary hearing to determine whether, under all the facts and circumstances of the case, a debtor is acting in bad faith or abusing the bankruptcy process and should be denied chapter 7 relief or, with the debtor's consent, the case should be converted to chapter 13 of the Bankruptcy Code.

To apply the means test, courts look at the debtor's current monthly income, which is the average income for the six months prior to filing, and compare it to the median income for that state. Specifically, "[c]urrent monthly income" is defined in §101(10A) as a monthly average of all the income received by the debtor (and the debtor's spouse in a joint case)—including regular contributions to household expenses made by other persons, but excluding benefits under the Social Security Act and certain victim payments—during the six-month period ending with the last day of the calendar month preceding the filing, as long as the debtor files a Schedule I (Statement of Current Income). Thus, for example, if a bankruptcy case were filed in March, as long as the debtor filed Schedule I, current monthly income would be the

---

86   Eugene R. Wedoff, *Major Consumer Bankruptcy Effects of BAPCPA*, 2007 Illinois L. Rev. 31.

IV. Application of §707(b) to Converted Cases

average monthly income received by the debtor during the preceding September through February.[87]

For example, the median annual income for a single wage-earner in Texas is $35,280. If the income is below the median, then chapter 7 remains an option. If the income exceeds the median, the remaining parts of the means test are triggered and must be considered.

Under §707(b)(2)(A)(i), two situations exist that may trigger the means test presumption of abuse. First, if the debtor has at least $182.50 in current monthly income available after the allowed deductions ($10,950 for five years), abuse is presumed regardless of the amount of the debtor's general unsecured debt. Second, if the debtor has at least $109.58 of such income ($6,575 for five years), abuse is presumed if the income is sufficient to pay at least 25 percent of the debtor's general unsecured debt over five years.

In summary, under the means test, a chapter 7 filing is presumed to be abusive if the debtor's monthly income, reduced by numerous allowances and living expenses, and multiplied by 60 (that is, over a five-year period), is greater than $10,950. If income thus adjusted is less than $6,575, there is no presumption of abuse, and the debtor is free to choose chapter 7, unless under the totality of the circumstances the debtor is nonetheless abusing the bankruptcy process. If adjusted income is between $6,575 and $10,950, abuse is presumed only if income exceeds 25 percent of nonpriority, unsecured debt in the case. An abusive chapter 7 filing is subject to dismissal or conversion.

The following chart, found in *In re Singletary,* 354 B.R. 455, 475 (Bankr. S.D. Tex. 2006), is especially helpful in deciphering the means test.

---

87   *Id.* However, if the debtor failed to file Schedule I, then the six-month period would end on the date that the court determines "current monthly income."

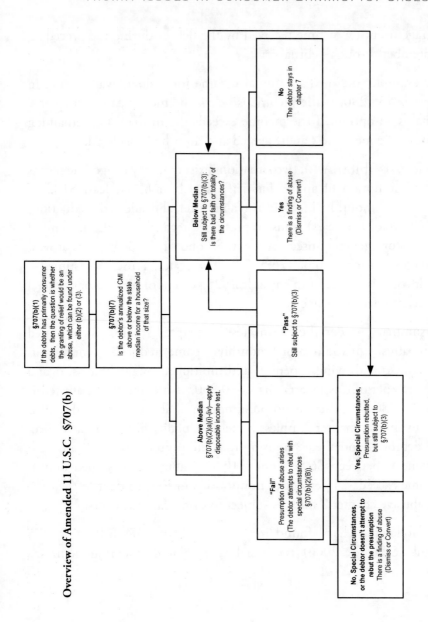

Overview of Amended 11 U.S.C. §707(b)

It is clear that the means test found in §707(b) is applicable to all cases filed under chapter 7. While a full discussion of the means test is outside the scope of these materials, the following table shows a few selected cases from the Bankruptcy Court for the Southern District of Texas:

Case Name	Cite	Judge	Holding
In re King	2008 WL 1808522 (Apr. 18, 2008)	Steen	The presumption of abuse arose under the means test. The UST's motion for summary judgment granted and the case dismissed.
In re Leary	2008 WL 1782636 (Apr. 16, 2008)	Steen	Debtors not allowed deduction for secured debts on surrendered property but allowed the deduction for vehicles as specified in the National and State Standards without reference to the IRM.
In re Brown	376 B.R. 601 (2007)	Bohm	Under the means test, debtors could not deduct, as "applicable monthly expense amount" specified under the Internal Revenue Service's (IRS's) National and Local Standards, a vehicle ownership expense for motor vehicles which they owned outright, but disposable income available to debtors warranted dismissal of case based on totality of circumstances.
In re Cadwallder	2007 WL 1864154 (June 28, 2007)	Steen	U.S. Trustee's motion to dismiss determined to be timely, and thus, prosecutable. Debtor's objections to motion related to inadequacy of the U.S. Trustee's statement under Bankruptcy Code §704(b) overruled, and the objection to the timeliness of the U.S. Trustee's motion to dismiss overruled.

IV. Application of §707(b) to Converted Cases

Case Name	Cite	Judge	Holding
In re Beacher	358 B.R. 917 (2007)	Isgur and Steen	In consolidated cases, debtors were not required to file Official Form where debts were not primarily consumer in nature, a nd dismissal of petition was not warranted on ground that debtors failed to file Official Form.
In re Singletary	354 B.R. 455 (2006)	Bohm	In applying the means test, the mere act of declaring an intent to surrender collateral on a Statement of Intention does not extinguish debtors' right to deduct those payments as being "scheduled as contractually due," but debtors may not deduct payments on collateral that already has been surrendered as of the motion date.
In re Copeland	2006 WL 2578877 (Sept. 5, 2006)	Clark	The court concluded that individual chapter 7 debtors with primarily business debts are required to file form B22A.
In re Hill	328 B.R. 490 (2005)	Isgur	In consolidated cases, court dismissed two cases on lack-of-need theory, as constituting a "substantial abuse" of provisions of chapter 7 where: (1) combined monthly income exceeded $13,600.00; and (2) debtors were making more than $300.00 in monthly voluntary contributions to retirement plan.

IV. Application of §707(b) to Converted Cases

After this lengthy lead-in, one substantial question remains: Does the "means test" apply in chapter 13 cases converted to chapter 7? At least part of the argument centers around the language in §707(b) that states "filed by an individual debtor under this chapter ." No cases in the Southern District of Texas or in the Fifth Circuit appear to address this question. However, a few other courts have ruled on this issue. In *In re Perfetto*, 361 B.R. 27 (Bankr. D. R.I. 2007), the debtor was required, upon conversion of her case, to complete and file the bankruptcy form implementing the statutory means test. This opinion is in accord with the consolidated opinion found in *In re Kerr*, 2007 WL 2119291 (Bankr. W.D. Wash. July 18, 2007). The court in the consolidated cases found in *In re Kellett*, 379 B.R. 332 (Bankr. D. Or. 2007), also agreed that generally debtors in cases converted to chapter 7 must file a Form 22A "Statement of Current Monthly Income and Means Test Calculation (Chapter 7)," but also concluded that this requirement could be waived in specific circumstances and so waived the requirement. However, *In re Fox*, 370 B.R. 639 (Bankr. D. N.J 2007), reached the opposite conclusion, determining that the "means test" applied only to those cases commenced under chapter 7 and excluded cases converted from other chapters.

IV. Application of §707(b) to Converted Cases

V.

Chapter 13 Plan Modifications

Although a full discussion of chapter 13 plan modifications is beyond the scope of this book, there are certain emerging issues that are demanding of careful analysis. For example, in *In re Meza*, 467 F.3d 874 (5th Cir. 2006), the court considered the interaction of §§1329(a) and 1329(b)(2). As the court observed, when considered together, those sections:

> show that, when a modification request is timely filed, the completion of the plan and eventual discharge of the debtor is stayed until the bankruptcy court is allowed to consider the modification on its merits. A contrary result would encourage gamesmanship on behalf of debtors and prevent them from repaying creditors "to the extent of [their] capabilit[ies]."

In *In re Murphy*, 474 F.3d 143 (4th Cir. 2007), the Fourth Circuit addressed two cases involving instances in which a chapter 13 trustee sought to modify a confirmed chapter 13 plan to increase the amount to be paid to the unsecured creditors. The U.S. Bankruptcy Court for the Eastern District of Virginia, Stephen S. Mitchell, J., 327 B.R. 760, granted the motion with respect to one debtor's plan and denied the motion with respect to the other debtor's plan. The chapter 13 trustee appealed. The U.S. District Court for the Eastern District of Virginia, Claude M. Hilton, J., affirmed. The Fourth

Circuit affirmed, holding that the refinancing of a home mortgage was not a substantial change in the financial condition, as required to modify a chapter 13 plan. Moreover, the court held that a sale of the debtor's condominium was a "substantial and unanticipated change" in the debtor's financial circumstances, and the proposed modification of the chapter 13 plan was warranted.

In *In re Nichols,* 440 F.3d 850 (6th Cir. 2006), the court noted that a post-confirmation plan modification could be approved, although it would likely cause a creditor to become undersecured. In that case, a modified chapter 13 plan proposed by the debtors to cure a post-confirmation default resulting from the debtor-husband's temporary loss of employment, under which the debtors proposed to use their disposable income first to cure a default in their mortgage payments and to delay any payment to a purchase-money motor vehicle lender for nearly one year, did not impair the lender's lien rights contrary to the Fifth Amendment. Moreover, the Sixth Circuit held that the bankruptcy court did not abuse its discretion in approving the modified chapter 13 plan. While this delay in payment would likely cause the lender to become slightly undersecured, the lender, as of the date of the hearing on the modified plan, was still protected by a slight equity cushion in the collateral. Moreover, the court found that the lender had already received a significant portion of the total amount due, having received plan payments alone of roughly $14,300 on the original $14,000 debt, and would receive most of what it bargained for at the start of the parties' relationship, including interest.

In *In re Disney,* 386 B.R. 292 (Bankr. D. Colo. 2008), the bankruptcy court granted a motion to reclassify certain claims and modify a chapter 13 plan. The court specifically held that a creditor could be bound by the debtor's post-confirmation modification of a chapter 13 plan. Moreover, the court held that a chapter 13 debtor may recharacterize an allowed secured claim post-confirmation following foreclosure or surrender of collateral and treat the resulting deficiency claim in the modified plan. The court further found that cause existed to reconsider the allowance of the creditor's claim. Thus, the debtor could modify his treatment of the creditor's claim under his plan to provide for the claim to be paid as an unsecured claim. Finally, the reclassification of a creditor's claim and modification of its treatment under a confirmed plan did not violate the creditor's due process rights.

In *In re Demske,* 372 B.R. 85 (Bankr. M.D. Fla. 2007), the court held that a lack of evidence as to how mortgage refinancing affected debtors' disposable income, either positively or negatively, prevented the court from granting the debtors' motion to modify the chapter 13 plan to pay off their creditors early with proceeds of mortgage refinancing. Moreover, in *In re Belcher,* 369 B.R. 465 (Bankr. E.D. Ark. 2007), the court found that the debtors could not modify their confirmed chapter 13 plan to provide that a lender's perfected purchase money security interest in a motor vehicle would be satisfied in full by payment of the insurance proceeds and the transfer of the wrecked vehicle to it, even though the wreck was an unanticipated event where the debtors had elected to retain the vehicle and pay the entire amount of the lender's claim plus interest under §1329. Lastly, in *In re Ireland,* 366 B.R. 27 (Bankr. W.D. Ark. 2007), the court found that the debtors, who had suffered a substantial reduction in income after filing their bankruptcy petition, were not prohibited by BAPCPA from modifying their chapter 13 plan after confirmation to reduce payments to the unsecured creditors, despite the contention that their "current monthly income" used to calculate the plan payments was permanently fixed at time they filed their bankruptcy petition.

V. Chapter 13 Plan Modifications

VI.

Dead Debtors – Can Your Creditors Follow You to the Great Beyond?

The death of debtors during the administration of their bankruptcy cases poses difficult bankruptcy questions. Debtor deaths leave the duties of a debtor's estate up in the air. For example, how does one square the debtor predischarge educational requirements with a premature death? The court, in *In re Robles,* 2007 WL 4410395 (Bankr. W.D. Tex. Dec. 13, 2007), observed, "A dead debtor is not getting into any more trouble—at least not in this world. And the probate estate is hardly in danger of profligacy either (though perhaps the estate's beneficiaries should be required to complete an instructional course in financial management as a precondition to their receiving their inheritance)." Moreover, in *In re Trembulak,* 362 B.R. 205 (Bankr. D. N.J. 2007), the court held that a debtor who died after filing a chapter 7 petition was exempted from BAPCPA's credit-counseling requirements, a rather sensible result.

As mentioned, even the administration of a bankruptcy case is made dramatically more difficult where the debtor has passed away. In *In re Lucio,* 251 B.R. 705 (Bankr. W.D. Tex. 2000), the court observed that a chapter 7 case may continue notwithstanding the death of the debtor. With that said, how is the case actually administered? In answering this question, the court has provide a helpful roadmap, at least where it comes to the first meeting of creditors under §341. The court held that a debtor's daughter could not appear at the first meeting of creditors as a substitute for the deceased debtor. Rather, the court held that the personal representative of the debtor's probate estate could appear on behalf of the debtor at the creditors' meeting, a ruling consistent with probate administration under state law. Acknowledging the increase in complexity and delays, the court reasoned that it might be necessary to continue the first meeting of creditors to afford the personal representative a fair opportunity to obtain necessary letters from the probate court.

In *In re Oliver,* 279 B.R. 69 (Bankr. W.D.N.Y. 2002), the court found that the failure of a chapter 7 debtor to appear at the first meeting of creditors, due to his death prior to that meeting, did not constitute a per se basis for dismissal of case. In support of its decision, the court found that the debtor was current in satisfying his obligations under Bankruptcy Code at time of his death and that the U.S. Trustee failed to show that the debtor's inability to appear at the meeting of creditors would have a meaningful adverse impact on the bankruptcy case administration. The court further observed that in order to obtain dismissal, the U.S. Trustee would have to show that the decedent's administrator was an inadequate substitute for the deceased chapter 7 debtor.

In *In re Peterson,* 897 F.2d 935 (8th Cir. 1990), the court addressed the question of exemptions in bankruptcy in the case of a deceased debtor. There the court held that under North Dakota law, the debtor's death eight months after filing a bankruptcy petition did not constitute an abandonment of the homestead exemption or cause the homestead to lapse and revert back to the bankruptcy estate. At least as to the homestead exemption, the court suggested the appropriate measuring date for eligibility to make the exemption is as of the time the debtor filed his bankruptcy petition.

Finally, in *In re Bauer,* 343 B.R. 234 (Bankr. W.D. Mo. 2006), the court found that the potential complications arising from the dual administration, after the chapter 7 debtors' deaths, of their bankruptcy and probate estates did not warrant dismissal of the bankruptcy cases or suspension of proceedings therein.

In summary, these cases have developed a sensible, pragmatic approach to the administration of the bankruptcy case where a debtor has passed away at some point after the commencement of the case. The key is to get meaningful notice of the death to the court, U.S. Trustee and other parties in interest. Moreover, mirroring the requirements under applicable state law, the debtor's attorney should identify the legal representative of the probate estate, usually identified by will or statute, and inform that person of the pending bankruptcy case and any responsibilities of the debtor left unfulfilled.

Appendix

Table of Cases

Appendix B

Case Summaries

I.D.1   *In re Cauthen*, 152 B.R. 149 (Bankr. S.D. Tex. 1993)

(1) debtor could not be granted discharge when current case was filed within six years of filing prior case in which debtor received discharge; (2) debtor's acts done to knowingly and wrongfully deprive plaintiffs of possession of their property without just cause created debt which was nondischargeable as willful and malicious injury caused by debtor; (3) debtor violated bankruptcy rule on sanctions when chapter 7 petition and response to plaintiffs' motion for relief from automobile stay were not well grounded in fact, were not warranted by existing law, and were filed for delay only; and (4) appropriate sanction was injunction against debtor's filing any bankruptcy petitions in violation of the law.

I.D.1   *In re Mayo*, 2007 WL 1074078
(Bankr. D. Md. Jan. 12, 2007)

"The Defendant commenced Case No. 00-22042-PM in this Court on November 13, 2000. On February 21, 2001, the Defendant received a Chapter 7 discharge in that case. The Defendant's current bankruptcy case was commenced on December 27, 2005, less than 8 years following the commencement of Case No. 00-22042-PM." Thus, the plaintiff objecting to the debtor's discharge prevailed.

I.D.1   *In re McKittrick*, **349 B.R. 569 (Bankr. W.D. Wis. 2006)**

Modifying the future eligibility of a debtor to receive a discharge in bankruptcy is, in general, simply part of Congress' power under the bankruptcy clause of the Constitution. Thus, the change from six to eight years between discharges affected the debtor where the statute was amended between her two cases.

I.D.2   *In re Bateman*, **515 F.3d 272 (4th Cir. 2008)**

(1) Code provision purporting to deny a discharge to chapter 13 debtor who previously received a discharge "in a case filed under Chapter 13 of this title during the 2-year period preceding the date of such order" had to be interpreted as barring debtor from obtaining a discharge in current chapter 13 case, not if debtor received a prior chapter 13 discharge by discharge order entered less than two years before order for relief in current case, but only if debtor received a discharge in prior case that was filed less than two years before order for relief in current case; and (2) debtor's inability to obtain discharge did not make him ineligible to file for chapter 13 relief or affect good faith of his petition or proposed plan.

I.D.2   *In re Capers*, **347 B.R. 169 (Bankr. D. S.C. 2006)**

Code provision added by BAPCPA, which rendered ineligible for discharge under chapter 13 any debtor who within four years of entry of order for relief in chapter 13 case had received discharge in "a case filed under chapter 7, 11, or 12 of this title," served to prevent chapter 13 debtor from obtaining a discharge under that chapter based on fact that, less than four years prior to order for relief, she had received chapter 7 discharge, notwithstanding that she received this prior chapter 7 discharge in case that was originally filed under chapter 13 and only later converted to one under chapter 7; even assuming that language of provision, interpreted literally, did not operate to disqualify debtor from obtaining a discharge under chapter 13, because case in which she obtained a prior bankruptcy discharge was originally "filed" under chapter 13, court had to reject such a "literal" application as clearly at odds with expressed congressional intent.

I.D.2   *In re Grice*, **373 B.R. 886 (Bankr. E.D. Wis. 2007)**

The bankruptcy case that chapter 13 debtor had previously filed had to be treated as having been filed under chapter 7, the chapter to which it was converted, and not under chapter 13, the chapter under which it was originally commenced, for purpose of deciding whether debtor was entitled to discharge.

I.D.2   *In re Grydzuk*, **353 B.R. 564 (Bankr. N.D. Ind. 2006)**

The discharge referred to in §1328(f)(1) precluding a chapter 13 discharge if the debtor has received a discharge in a case during the prior four-year period refers to the chapter under which the discharge was actually entered, rather than the chapter under which the earlier case was initiated. Here the debtor converted the previous case from 13 to 7.

I.D.2   *In re Khan*, **2006 WL 3716036 (D. Md. Dec. 14, 2006)**

"The absence of a like prohibition on serial filings of Chapter 7 and Chapter 13 petitions, combined with the evident care with which Congress fashioned these express prohibitions, convinces us that Congress did not intend categorically to foreclose the benefit of Chapter 13 reorganization to a debtor who previously has filed for Chapter 7 relief."

I.D.2   *In re Knighton*, **355 B.R. 922 (Bankr. M.D. Ga. 2006)**

Under statute barring discharge in debtor's pending chapter 13 case if debtor received prior discharge in a case filed under chapter 7 during four-year period preceding the date of the order for relief in pending case, look-back period runs from filing date of prior case to filing date of pending case. Chapter 13 debtor was eligible for discharge upon completion of her pending case, given that more than four years had passed between filing of debtor's prior case to filing of pending case.

I.D.2   ***In re Sours*, 350 B.R. 261 (Bankr. E.D. Va. 2006)**

"[i]t is clear to this Court that a converted case relates back to the initial filing date for all purposes, including matters relating to discharge. Section 348(a) provides that 'conversion from a case under one chapter of this title to a case under another chapter of this title constitutes an order for relief under the chapter to which the case is converted.' 11 U.S.C. §348(a). Thus, the Court agrees with the United States Trustee that §348(a) mandates that a case which has been converted to Chapter 7 from Chapter 13, such as the Debtors' Prior Case, is deemed to be 'filed under' Chapter 7 on the date on which the Chapter 13 was filed. Accordingly, this Court also finds that Section 348(a) mandates that it is the original filing date of a case, not the conversion date, which controls the running of the time-bar for discharge purposes. Therefore, the Debtors are subject to the four-year time restriction of §1328(f)(1) and are not eligible to receive a discharge in the Pending Case."

I.D.2   ***In re Ybarra*, 359 B.R. 702 (Bankr. S.D. Ill. 2007)**

Phrase "in a case filed," as used in bankruptcy statute barring debtors from obtaining a discharge under chapter 13 if, within four years prior to order for relief in current chapter 13 case, they have previously received a discharge in case filed under chapter 7, 11 or 12, was not limited in its application only to chapter under which petition was initially filed in this prior case, but also included the chapter under which petition was deemed filed if prior case was converted from one chapter to another prior to entry of discharge order; accordingly, this four-year "look back" period applied to debtors who, prior to commencement of their current chapter 13 case, had previously received discharge in chapter 7, though this chapter 7 discharge was entered in case that debtors had commenced by filing petition under chapter 13, and that was deemed to be filed under chapter 7 only when case was converted.

I.D.2 *Sanders v. Carroll,* **2008 WL 275678 (E.D. Mich. Jan. 31, 2008)**

"The overwhelming majority of bankruptcy courts that have addressed the start and/or end date of the look-back periods in §1328(f) have held that, to give effect to the plain meaning of the statutory language, the look-back periods referred to in §1328(f) begin with the filing of the debtor's first bankruptcy case as opposed to the issuance of a discharge in that first case. This Court finds the reasoning and result of this overwhelming majority of bankruptcy courts to be more persuasive than that of the bankruptcy court here."

I.D.3 *In re Griffin,* **352 B.R. 475 (B.A.P. 8th Cir. 2006)**

Debtor who files chapter 7 case within six years of petition date of earlier chapter 13 case will not be denied chapter 7 discharge if debtor, in that chapter 13 case, paid to trustee for distribution under debtor's plan an amount equal to 70 percent of allowed unsecured claims and court finds that plan was proposed by debtor in good faith and was debtor's best effort, or if debtor paid to trustee for distribution under plan an amount which totaled at least 100 percent of allowed unsecured claims.

I.D.3 *In re Perez,* **339 B.R. 385 (Bankr. S.D. Tex. 2006)**

(1) adequate protection payments to real estate lien holders are not "payments made under a proposed plan" that chapter 13 trustee is statutorily required to hold until plan is confirmed;   (2) adequate protection payments which chapter 13 trustee was authorized to make preconfirmation to mortgagee did not have to be in some amount that was less than debtor-mortgagors' regular monthly payments;

(3) debtors lacked standing to assert that local rule which required that residential mortgage payments must be made through trustee, in accordance with the Home Mortgage Payment Procedures, violated the anttimodification provision of chapter 13; (4) trustee's disbursement of home mortgage payments to mortgagee did not violate priority provision; and (5) debtors would not be allowed to make direct payments on their home mortgage debt.

I.D.3   ***Tidewater Finance Co. v. Williams*, 498 F.3d 249 (4th Cir. 2007)**

"[T]he six-year waiting period in §727(a)(8) is [not] a limitations period that the bankruptcy court should have equitably tolled during [debtor's] Chapter 13 proceedings."

I.D.4   ***In re Bateman*, 341 B.R. 540 (Bankr. D. Md. 2006)**

Provision of BAPCPA that prevented court from granting chapter 13 debtors a discharge of debts provided for in their plans if debtors had received a discharge in another case within two- or four-year "look back" periods was not eligibility provision, and mere fact that debtors may have been barred from obtaining discharge in their current chapter 13 cases did not make them ineligible for chapter 13 relief.

I.D.4   ***In re Bateman*, 515 F.3d 272 (4th Cir. 2008)**

(1) Code provision purporting to deny a discharge to chapter 13 debtor who previously received a discharge "in a case filed under Chapter 13 of this title during the 2-year period preceding the date of such order" had to be interpreted as barring debtor from obtaining a discharge in current chapter 13 case, not if debtor received a prior chapter 13 discharge by discharge order entered less than two years before order for relief in current case, but only if debtor received a discharge in prior case that was filed less than two years before order for relief in current case; and (2) debtor's inability to obtain discharge did not make him

ineligible to file for chapter 13 relief or affect good faith of his petition or proposed plan.

I.D.4   ***In re Graves*, 2007 WL 1075108 (Bankr. D. Md. Jan. 19, 2007)**

"Applying these standards to the language of Section 1328, the Court concludes that the application of the plain meaning rule results in the adoption of the 'filing date to filing date' interpretation of Section 1328(f)(2). The 'filing date to filing date' approach implements Section 1328 the way it is written. Section 1328(f)(2) prohibits a debtor from receiving a discharge 'if the debtor has received a discharge…in a case filed under chapter 13…during the 2-year period' preceding the date of the order for relief of the current case. The 'filing date to filing date' interpretation gives effect to the logical sequence of the language used. Each subsequent clause modifies the immediately preceding clause. All words are given effect. No punctuation needs to be added or deleted."

I.D.4   ***In re Lewis*, 339 B.R. 814 (Bankr. S.D. Ga. 2006)**

Provision of BAPCPA that prevented court from granting chapter 13 debtors a discharge of debts provided for in their plans if debtors had received a discharge in another case within two- or four-year "look back" periods was not eligibility provision, and mere fact that debtors were barred from obtaining discharge in their current chapter 13 cases did not, standing alone, affect debtors' eligibility for chapter 13 relief.

I.D.4   ***In re Ward*, 370 B.R. 812 (Bankr. D. Neb. 2007)**

Chapter 13 debtors discharge prohibition period of §1328(f) commenced upon the filing of the first chapter 13 case.

I.D.4   ***In re West*, 352 B.R. 482 (Bankr. E.D. Ark. 2006)**

"A Debtor is not entitled to a chapter 13 discharge under §1328(f)(2) if the Debtor has received a discharge in a case filed under chapter 13 within two years of the current case's filing." Therefore, a debtor who received a discharge in a chapter 13 case filed more than two years before the current case is entitled to a discharge. The court determined that the two-year period was measured from the filing dates of the two cases, and not from the discharge of the first and the filing of the second.

I.D.5   *In re Bateman,* **515 F. 3d 272 (4th Cir. 2008)**

The debtor is not precluded from filing in good faith a new chapter 13 bankruptcy case even though he may be ineligible for a discharge under §1328(f).

I.D.5   *In re Godwin,* **2007 WL 4191729 (Bankr. M.D.N.C. Nov. 21, 2007)**

"While the Court agrees that a Chapter 7 discharge is not a per se bar to a debtor's ability to proceed under Chapter 13, the Court finds the reasoning of those courts that disallow a debtor to receive two discharges in the same case to be highly persuasive…The Debtors should not be allowed to do indirectly, through conversion, what they cannot do directly by filing a new Chapter 13. Therefore, as a condition to granting the Motion to Convert, the Debtors must file a Motion to Revoke the Chapter 7 Discharge that was granted."

I.D.5   *In re Sanders,* **368 B.R. 634 (Bankr. E.D. Mich. 2007)**

The court acknowledged that the debtor who filed his chapter 13 case within four years of his previous chapter 7 case was statutorily barred from receiving a chapter 13 discharge. However, this did not preclude confirmation of the debtor's proposed plan, it was otherwise confirmable.

I.E   *In re Fuller,* **2005 WL 3454699 (Bankr. W.D. Pa. Dec. 16, 2005)**

"Debtor does not understand that the two educational requirements represent two distinct requirements with different timing. The credit counseling requirement must be completed prior to the bankruptcy filing in order for an individual to be eligible to file a bankruptcy Petition. The financial management course must be completed 'after filing the petition,'" thus the certification was stricken and the debtor ordered to complete the financial management course.

I.E and   *In re Trembulak,* **362 B.R. 205**
E.3.b   **(Bankr. D. N.J. 2007)**

"[C]learly the Debtor herein cannot participate in an instructional course on personal financial management and obviously such a course will not aid the Debtor in avoiding future financial distress. It seems palpably obvious that if a financial management course would be meaningless for an 81 year old, hearing-impaired debtor, suffering from prostate cancer, then such a course would likewise offer even less benefit to a deceased debtor."

I.E.3.c   *In re Hall,* **347 B.R. 532 (Bankr. N.D. W.Va. 2006)**

Chapter 7 debtor was entitled to a "disability" waiver of BAPCPA's requirement that he complete a postpetition instructional course concerning personal financial management where, although debtor was capable of some mobility, as he was able to visit his attorney's office, the courtroom, and the location of his prepetition credit counseling, debtor demonstrated a severe physical impairment, in that he was 81 years old, hearing impaired, and limited to a scooter for mobility, and he suffered from serious health issues, including prostate cancer, debtor made a reasonable effort to complete the instructional course concerning personal financial management, but was unable to do so due to a combination of his limited mental capacity, hearing impairment, and other physical impairments, and the course thus was of no benefit to debtor in avoiding future financial distress.

I.E.3.c   *In re Howard,* **359 B.R. 589 (Bankr. E.D.N.C. 2007)**

Chapter 13 debtor suffered from a "disability" within the meaning of the Bankruptcy Code and, thus, was exempt from the prepetition credit counseling requirement, where debtor was required to travel to obtain dialysis treatments, debtor had been hospitalized, suffered cardiac arrest, and placed on life support for approximately 14 days, and since his release from the hospital, debtor had suffered from short-term memory loss, hearing loss, and limited mobility.

I.E.3.c   *In re Jarrell,* **364 B.R. 899 (Bankr. N.D. Tex. 2007)**

Chapter 7 debtor, who had a mental illness, had the requisite "incapacity" to justify a waiver of the Bankruptcy Code's prepetition credit counseling requirement; debtor's psychologist testified that, while debtor could identify specific assets or debts, he did not understand, and could not reasonably be expected to make decisions that required him to understand, the relationship between the two.

I.E.3.c   *In re Petit-Louis,* **344 B.R. 696 (Bankr. S.D. Fla. 2006)**

Debtor was entitled to waiver of credit counseling requirement imposed by BAPCPA, based on fact that when petition was filed, there were no approved counseling agencies in district that offered credit counseling in Creole. The bankruptcy court held that where the debtor, for whom the filing fee had been waived, had only limited English and the U.S. Trustee could not provide either a translator or Creole speaking counselors, the counseling would be of little benefit and thus the requirement was waived.

I.E.3.c   *In re Tulper,* **345 B.R. 322 (Bankr. D. Colo. 2006)**

Chapter 13 debtors were entitled to a permanent, "disability" exemption from BAPCPA's credit counseling requirement where it was apparent that debtors were severely physically impaired, as debtor-wife was not very ambulatory because she was tethered to a breathing apparatus and was wheelchair-bound and debtor-husband was virtually deaf and his hands and feet were disabled; debtors made reasonable efforts to address credit counseling by conferring with an accountant and an attorney, and debtors, though competent and lucid, were unable to sufficiently comprehend information necessary to formulate a budget and analyze finances because of their physical condition, and so were unable to participate in a meaningful way in any credit counseling briefing.

I.F   *In re Ventura*, 375 B.R. 103 (Bankr. E.D.N.Y. 2007)

"Cause" existed to dismiss debtor's chapter 7 case where debtor, after his case was randomly selected for audit pursuant to provision added by BAPCPA, failed to fulfill statutory duties of cooperating with chapter 7 trustee and auditor, of surrendering recorded information to chapter 7 trustee and auditor, or of appearing for examination, with result that trustee was unable to administer case and auditor was unable to conduct audit.

I.F.   *In re Kelton*, 389 B.R. 812 (Bankr. S.D. Ga. 2008)

Chapter 13 debtor's understatement of current monthly income on Form 22C by $1,204.88 was a "material" mistatement, as reported in audit, even though disposable income would still remain negative. U.S. Trustee's proposed rule 2004 exam to address anomalies in schedules was legititate use of rule 2004.

I.F   *Lampf v. Gilbertson*, 501 U.S. 350 (1991)

(1) statute of limitations applicable to actions under §10(b) is the one-and-three-year provisions of the Securities Exchange Act and Securities Act for causes of action which they specifically provide for, and (2) equitable tolling is not applicable.

II   *In re Bellamy*, 379 B.R. 86 (Bankr. D. Md. 2007)

"After examining Section 1326(b) and the cases which have interpreted it, this court reaches the conclusion that the statute does require the Trustee to pay in full any allowed and outstanding administrative claim [including attorney fees] as a part of any distribution, before distributions may be made to other claimants, except possibly holders of domestic support obligations entitled to priority under Section 507(a)(1)."

II   *In re Bernales*, 345 B.R. 206 (Bankr. C.D. Cal. 2006)

(1) BAPCPA did not preempt state law on unauthorized practice of law; (2) petition preparer engaged in "unauthorized practice of law," *inter alia*, by advising its debtor-client in e-mail message that most bankruptcy courts allowed debtors to pay filing fees in installments; (3) as sanction, court would require petition preparer to disgorge any compensation received, as well as to pay separate $2,000 fines to debtor and to U.S. Trustee; and (4) petition preparer would be permanently enjoined from acting in such capacity in the Central District of California.

II.A.1   *In re Montemayor Trucking Inc.*, 2006 WL 3545459 (Bankr. S.D. Tex. Dec. 8, 2006)

"A debtor's attorney will be entitled to attorneys fees that will be paid as an administrative expense in only two circumstances: (1) if the debtor is a debtor in possession in chapter 11 and therefore exercises the authority of a trustee, and (2) if the case is a chapter 12 or a chapter 13 case. There is no other provision in the Bankruptcy Code for allowance of fees for a debtor's attorney. Therefore... applicant is not entitled to an award of attorneys fees for services rendered subsequent to the date that the case was converted [from Chapter 11 to Chapter 7] and his client, the Debtor, ceased to exercise the authority of a trustee."

II.A.1   *In re Smith*, 2006 WL 3627149 (8th Cir. Dec. 14, 2006)

"The bankruptcy court's order instructing the trustee to withhold attorney's fees...in other bankruptcy cases as sanctions for [attorney's] continued violation of an earlier court order" was affirmed.

II.A.2   *In re Chapter 13 Fee Applications*, 2006 WL 2850115
(Bankr. S.D. Tex. Oct. 3, 2006)

The Southern District of Texas increased the fixed fee
amount of chapter 13 attorney's fees. "The maximum fixed
fee for chapter 13 cases filed after entry of this Order is
$3,085.00, including all expenses other than the filing fee.
For cases dismissed before confirmation or within 120 days
after confirmation, the maximum fixed fee is $2,700.00."

II.A.2   *In re Eliapo*, 468 F.3d 592 (9th Cir. 2006)

Issue of whether attorney for chapter 13 debtors was entitled
to compensation for work involving debtors' vehicle loan
depended upon the factual record, which had not clearly
been fully developed, and therefore issue, which was not
raised before bankruptcy appellate panel (BAP), did not
fall within "exceptional circumstance" exception to general
rule providing for waiver of issue not raised before BAP
and was waived for purposes of further review by court of
appeals on attorney's appeal challenging denial of requested
compensation.

II.A.2   *In re Mayer*, 2006 WL 2850451
(Bankr. D. Kan. Oct. 2, 2006)

The District of Kansas increased the presumptive attorney
fee amount. The court concluded that "the increased
workload and responsibilities of lawyers filing chapter 13
cases in the wake of BAPCPA merit an increase in the
presumptive fee from $2,000 to $2,500."

II.A.2   *In re McNally*, 2006 WL 2348687
(Bankr. D. Colo. Aug. 10, 2006)

"In this District, we have determined the Presumptively
Reasonable Fee structure is a more efficient and effective
procedure than examining the intricacies of every case. Our
current process has worked well, but will need tweaking,
both as a result of BAPCPA and possibly some based on
our collective experience of working under it for a few
years. These things are still a work-in-process."

II.A.2   *In re Mullings*, **2006 WL 2130648 (Bankr. E.D. Okla. July 26, 2006)**

"Effective August 15, 2006, in all cases filed or converted to a case under Chapter 13 of the Bankruptcy Code, the presumptive attorney fee shall be $3,750.00 in individual and small business cases. This will not eliminate the necessity of attorneys to continue to keep contemporaneous time records that identify the work performed. In some situations the Court will still consider reduction or disgorgement of fees when the professional work does not meet the high standards set by this Court. Upon proper application, the Court may consider enhancement of fees above the presumptive fee."

II.A.2   *In re Murray*, **348 B.R. 917 (Bankr. M.D. Ga. 2006)**

"...Administrative Order of January 3, 2005 shall be amended to reflect the following changes: Effective as to cases filed on or after August 1, 2006, an attorney for a Chapter 13 debtor or joint debtors (for purposes of the following paragraphs (a) through (c), "Debtor") need not file an initial fee application if the fee sought to be paid per case is $2,500.00 or less; provided, however, that...."

II.A.3   *In re DeSardi*, **340 B.R. 790 (Bankr. S.D. Tex. 2006)**

Court held that administrative expenses in the form of adequate protection payments to purchase money creditors outranked a debtor's attorney's fees based on protections found in §507(b) and sustained the creditors' objections.

II.A.3   *In re Dispirito*, **371 B.R. 695 (Bankr. D. N.J. 2007)**

"Adequate protection payments to automobile lenders have priority over claims for attorneys fees made by counsel for Chapter 13 debtors."

II.A.3   *In re Erwin*, **376 B.R. 897 (Bankr. C.D. Ill. 2007)**

"The equal payment provision, directed at debtors and not Chapter 13 trustees, does not require a trustee's monthly payments to secured creditors to be perfectly equal in amount. Trustees may continue to pay debtors' attorney fees on an accelerated basis despite the resulting increase in secured creditor payments once the attorney is fully paid."

II.A.4 *In re Johnson*, **344 B.R. 104 (B.A.P. 9th Cir. 2006)**

A chapter 13 debtor's obligation for the postconfirmation fees of his bankruptcy counsel would not be discharged upon the completion of the debtor's payments under the plan and the entry of an order of discharge. The debtor's confirmed plan specifically provided that such postconfirmation fees would be paid by the debtor directly and would not be discharged upon the entry of an order of discharge. This plan provision, which enabled the debtor to complete his plan payments without reducing or stretching out payments to other creditors, was not inconsistent with any provision of title 11.

II.B *In re Hudson*, **2007 WL 4219421**
(Bankr. C.D. Ill. Nov. 27, 2007)

Attorney fees that the debtor was ordered to pay, and which were incurred in a paternity/support proceeding, are non-dischargeable because they are considered in the nature of support.

II.B *In re Murphy*, **346 B.R. 79 (Bankr. S.D.N.Y. 2006)**

The bankruptcy court held that: (1) on *ex parte* application by mortgagee for "comfort order," to effect that temporary stay arising in chapter 13 case filed by repeat filer had terminated 30 days after order for relief, bankruptcy court's function was limited to "confirming" an objective fact, that stay had terminated pursuant to provision of BAPCPA; and (2) to extent that creditor filing this application for "comfort order" also sought to recover attorney fees that it incurred, it had to file separate application for such fees on notice to parties affected.

II.B   ***In re Padilla*, 379 B.R. 643 (Bankr. S.D. Tex. 2007)**

In a series of consolidated chapter 13 cases, the debtors challenged fees and expenses charged by home mortgage lenders where the lenders failed to file reimbursement applications with the court. According to the court, the failure to comply with rule 2016(a) or the imposition of reimbursable expenses beyond those allowed by contract and applicable nonbankruptcy law prepetition not only violated the rule but also violated the order confirming the chapter 13 cases, entitling the debtors to relief against the creditors, including costs and fees.

II.B   ***In re Ryker*, 2007 WL 2138590 (3d Cir. July 27, 2007)**

Mortgage-holders were entitled to attorneys fees incurred in connection with the sale of commercial property upon which chapter 13 debtor defaulted.

III   ***In re Allen*, 378 B.R. 151 (Bankr. N.D. Tex. 2007)**

Credit-counseling requirement added by BAPCPA pertains only to an individual who is the subject of a voluntary bankruptcy case and does not apply to putative debtors who are the subject of involuntary petitions.

III   ***In re Diloreto*, 2008 WL 141922 (Bankr. E.D. Pa. Jan. 11, 2008)**

"The express language of section 109(h)(1) makes clear that the credit counseling requirement applies only to voluntary petitions…[However,] the petitioning creditor here did not comply with the service requirements of Rule 7004 when Federal Express delivered the involuntary petition to the putative debtor." The debtor's request for a dismissal was granted.

III.B.1   ***In re Bricksin*, 346 B.R. 497 (Bankr. N.D. Cal. 2006)**

While debtors' initial credit counseling session, occurring more than 180 days prior to petition date, was technically insufficient to satisfy BAPCPA's credit counseling requirement, debtors' conduct, after they obtain this initial counseling, in participating in and performing under plan developed by counselor for several months until they were eventually forced to file bankruptcy petition, as their counselor had initially recommended, qualified as ongoing "credit counseling," that extended into statutory 180-day period, and that satisfied requirements.

III.B.1   *In re Dyer,* **381 B.R. 200 (Bankr. W.D.N.C. 2007)**

Chapter 7 case filed by debtors who had obtained credit counseling more than 180 days prepetition had to be dismissed based upon debtors' ineligibility to be bankruptcy debtors; debtors could not invoke bankruptcy statute authorizing court to enter "necessary or appropriate" orders or equitable doctrine of substantial performance in order to avoid consequences of their failure to comply with plain terms of "credit counseling" requirement.

III.B.1   *In re Enloe,* **373 B.R. 123 (Bankr. D. Colo. 2007)**

Mere fact that debtors, as result of their attorney's error, did not file for chapter 7 relief until 189 days after they received credit counseling did not warrant dismissal of case

III.B.1   *In re Gaddis,* **2007 WL 1610783**
(Bankr. D. Kan. June 4, 2007)

Debtor's receiving credit counseling 186 days before filing bankruptcy petition does not satisfy §109(h).

III.B.1   *In re Giles,* **361 B.R. 212 (Bankr. D. Utah 2007)**

Debtors who obtained credit counseling 182 days prior to commencement of their chapter 13 case did not satisfy their obligation, as prerequisite to being eligible for bankruptcy relief, to receive such counseling within 180 days of filing, and court had no discretion to excuse debtors' noncompliance on theory that they had complied with spirit of credit counseling requirement. On motion of trustee, case dismissed.

III.B.1   *In re Hess*, 347 B.R. 489 (Bankr. D. Vt. 2006)

(1) mere fact that debtors, due to their inability to provide required proof of prepetition credit counseling or to qualify for waiver or exemption, were ineligible for bankruptcy relief did not necessarily mean that court had to dismiss their petitions; (2) court would not dismiss chapter 7 case filed by debtor who, while checking box on petition indicating that he had obtained the requisite prepetition credit counseling, was unable to provide certificate from credit counseling agency because agency was not an approved agency at time; and (3) court would not dismiss chapter 7 case filed by debtor whose petition was mistakenly filed, while her attorney was absent from law office to undergo emergency medical procedure, before debtor could obtain prepetition credit counseling.   "[U]nder the totality of the circumstances presented, [the Court] has discretion to allow the cases to proceed, notwithstanding the procedural eligibility defect."

III.B.1   *In re Meza*, 2007 WL 1821416
(E.D. Cal. June 25, 2007)

Debtor's bankruptcy petition substantially complied with the eligibility requirements of §109(h) despite debtor receiving debt counseling prior to enactment of BAPCPA and filing petition after BAPCPA's enactment.

III.B.1   *In re Williams*, 359 B.R. 590 (Bankr. E.D.N.C. 2007)

"Section 109(h) does provide several exceptions for debtors who are unable to complete their credit counseling for various reasons prior to their filing. However, it does not provide an alternative for those who complete their credit counseling more than 180 days prior to their filing."

III.B.3.a   *In re Barbaran*, 365 B.R. 333 (Bankr. D. D.C. 2007)

The court rejected its prior rulings and stated that the use of the term "date" in §109(h) represents the moment of the filing of the petition rather than the day.

III.B.3.a *In re Cole*, 347 B.R. 70 (Bankr. E.D. Tenn. 2006)

In specifying that debtor must obtain credit counseling during the 180-day period "preceding the date" that petition was filed, Congress plainly precluded debtors from filing for bankruptcy on same date that credit counseling was obtained.   "[S]ection 109(h)(1)'s 180-day period preceding the date of filing of the petition does not include the date upon which a debtor's bankruptcy petition is filed."

III.B.3.a *In re Francisco*, 386 B.R. 854 (Bankr. D. N.M. 2008), *rev'd*, 390 B.R. 700 (B.A.P. 10th Cir. 2008)

"A debtor must obtain the budget and credit counseling prior to the date-day-of the filing of the petition." The result is that the case must be dismissed and not stricken. (OVERRULED)

III.B.3.a *In re Francisco*, 390 B.R. 700 (B.A.P. 10th Cir. 2008)

Overruling lower court determination and held that credit counseling requirement is satisfied when an individual debtor obtains credit counseling on the same day as, but prior to, the filing of the bankruptcy petition.

III.B.3.a *In re Gossett*, 369 B.R. 361 (Bankr. N.D. Ill. 2007)

Debtor who obtains the required prepetition credit counseling briefing on the same day as the date upon which a bankruptcy petition is filed does not comply with the statutory directive that he or she obtain a briefing "during the 180-day period preceding the date of filing of the petition" and, therefore, is not eligible to be a debtor under title 11; phrase "180-day period preceding the date of filing of the petition" does not include the date upon which a debtor's bankruptcy petition is filed.

III.B.3.a *In re Mills*, 341 B.R. 106 (Bankr. D. D.C. 2006), *abrogated by In re Barbaran*, 365 B.R. 333 (Bankr. D. D.C. 2007)

(1) under BAPCPA, debtor must obtain credit counseling not just some hours, minutes or seconds prior to filing petition, but at least one calendar day prior to petition date; and (2) petition filed by ineligible debtor was not void *ab initio*, but gave rise to case and to automatic stay for limited purpose of allowing court to assess debtor's eligibility and whether it could exercise subject matter jurisdiction over case. (ABROGATED by *Barbaran*)

III.B.3.a *In re Murphy*, 342 B.R. 671 (Bankr. D. D.C. 2006)

The court held that to meet the requirements of §109(h), the debtor must receive the credit counseling at least the day before the filing, not on the date of the filing.

III.B.3.b *In re Francisco*, 390 B.R. 700 (B.A.P. 10th Cir. 2008)

Overruling lower court determination and held that credit counseling requirement is satisfied when an individual debtor obtains credit counseling on the same day as, but prior to, the filing of the bankruptcy petition.

III.B.3.b *In re Hudson*, 352 B.R. 391 (Bankr. D. Md. 2006)

Chapter 13 debtor who obtained credit counseling on same day as his bankruptcy petition was filed, but prior to the filing of petition, satisfied statutory requirement that he obtain such counseling "during the 180-day period preceding the date of filing of the petition."

III.B.3.b *In re Moore*, 359 B.R. 665 (Bankr. E.D. Tenn. 2006)

"11 U.S.C. §109(h)(1) requires a debtor to receive a credit counseling briefing...prior to the moment of filing the petition, so long as the 180-day outside limit is otherwise met...It is clear that §109(h)(1) governs not the period of time for doing an act after a bankruptcy case is commenced but rather describes the requisite time for taking a step to establish eligibility to file a case in the first instance, much like the time for filing a complaint to satisfy a statute of limitations."

III.B.3.b *In re Spears*, **355 B.R. 116 (Bankr. E.D. Wis. 2006)**

Debtor who obtained credit counseling prior to, but on same day as, the filing of her bankruptcy petition satisfied requirement imposed by BAPCPA that she obtain credit counseling "during the 180-day period preceding the date of filing of the petition."

III.B.3.b *In re Swanson*, **2006 WL 3782906 (Bankr. D. Idaho Dec. 21, 2006)**

"The term 'date of filing' as found in §109(h) refers to the specific calendar day and time the petition was filed... Here, the credit briefing Debtor obtained prior to filing but on the same day he filed his bankruptcy petition complied with §109(h)."

III.B.3.b *In re Toccaline*, **2006 WL 2081517 (Bankr. D. Conn. July 17, 2006)**

Agreeing with *In re Warren*, the court found that credit counseling on the day of the filing was sufficient to meet the requirements of 11 U.S.C. §109(h)(1).

III.B.3.b *In re Warren*, **339 B.R. 475 (Bankr. E.D. Ark. 2006)**

Requirement that the putative debtor obtain credit counseling prior to filing referred not just to calendar date on which petition was filed, but to particular year, month, date and time of day that petition was filed, so as to require only that credit counseling precede the filing of petition, not that it precede it by at least one calendar date.

III.C.1.a *Clippard v. Bass*, **365 B.R. 131 (W.D. Tenn. 2007)**

Eligibility to be debtor is not jurisdictional, and until bankruptcy court determines eligibility, a bankruptcy case filed by ineligible debtor actually exists, which cannot thereafter be deemed a nullity by simply striking case as if it never existed.

III.C.1.a *In re Hoshan,* **2008 WL 81994 (E.D. Pa. Jan. 7, 2008).**

"The credit counseling requirement is not jurisdictional... The appellant did not get credit counseling until after she had filed her petition, and she did not seek an exigent circumstances waiver. Her family situation, while difficult, does not rise to the level of those cases in which courts avoid manifest injustice by waiving the credit counseling requirements."

III.C.1.a *In re Manalad,* **360 B.R. 288 (Bankr. C.D. Cal. 2007)**

Finding that the credit counseling requirement was not jurisdictional in nature and did not necessarily mandate dismissal, the court determined factors pertinent to court's determination as to whether bankruptcy case should be dismissed include: (1) whether debtor has reasonable explanation for not participating in budget and credit counseling within 180 days prior to filing bankruptcy petition; (2) whether debtor participates in budget and credit counseling once debtor learns that it is necessary; and (3) whether it is determined at budget and credit counseling session that debtor's debts could not have been paid outside of bankruptcy.

III.C.1.a *In re Mendez,* **367 B.R. 109 (B.A.P. 9th Cir. 2007)**

Addressing an issue of apparent first impression at the appellate level, pre-bankruptcy credit counseling is not a jurisdictional prerequisite but, instead, is a matter of individual eligibility, subject to principles of waiver and estoppel.

III.C.1.a *In re Seaman,* **340 B.R. 698 (Bankr. E.D.N.Y. 2006)**

While finding the eligibility to be a debtor is not jurisdictional, the court determined that the appropriate remedy for failure to obtain credit counseling was dismissal rather than striking the petition because until the eligibility is determined, the case proceeds and thus cannot be a nullity. Further, dismissal is appropriate because "[d]ismissal is the result in nearly all of the cases filed by petitioners who are ineligible under other subsections of Section 109."

III.C.1.a *Warren v. Wirum*, **378 B.R. 640 (N.D. Cal. 2007)**

District court determined that the credit counseling requirement was not jurisdictional in nature.

III.C.1.b *In re Giles*, **361 B.R. 212 (Bankr. D. Utah 2007)**

The court held that it lacked jurisdiction over the debtor's case, where the debtor failed to comply with the credit counseling requirement imposed by §109(h).

III.C.1.b *In re Valdez*, **335 B.R. 801 (Bankr. S.D. Fla. 2005)**

Where petitioner was ineligible for failure to obtain credit counseling and failing to meet the standards for a waiver, the status of "debtor" was never conveyed. Finding eligibility to be jurisdictional, the court would "not consider this a dismissed case in which the individual was the debtor, for the purposes of denying the imposition of the automatic stay in subsequently filed case."

III.C.2 *In re Salazar*, **339 B.R. 622 (Bankr. S.D. Tex. 2006)**

Where putative debtor files a petition but is not eligible for bankruptcy relief due to failure to obtain credit counseling, such filing does not give rise to bankruptcy case or entitle debtor, even temporarily until eligibility determination is made, to protections of automatic stay.

III.C.2.a *In re Elmendorf*, **345 B.R. 486 (Bankr. S.D.N.Y. 2006)**

Court found that filing of bankruptcy petition without first obtaining credit counseling, which renders debtor ineligible for bankruptcy relief, does not trigger protections of automatic stay and that the bankruptcy court may decide, on case-by-case basis, whether to strike petition filed in violation of credit counseling requirement.

III.C.2.b *In re Brown*, **342 B.R. 248 (Bankr. D. Md. 2006)**

Filing of chapter 13 petition by debtor who, as result of her failure to obtain credit counseling prepetition or to file certification of exigent circumstances that was satisfactory to court, was not eligible for chapter 13 relief was not a mere nullity, but gave rise to automatic stay that remained in effect until bankruptcy court denied debtor's request for waiver of prepetition credit counseling requirement and dismissed case.

III.C.2.b *In re Hawkins,* **340 B.R. 642 (Bankr. D. D.C. 2006)**

"Section 362(b)(21) must be read as implying that the automatic stay is in effect while the court makes this threshold determination of jurisdiction. A petition by an ineligible debtor gives rise to a case in this limited sense and to an automatic stay until the case is dismissed. In other words, §362 must be read as giving rise to an automatic stay when a petition is asserted to be filed under §§301, 302, or 303."

III.D *In re Hubbard,* **333 B.R. 377 (Bankr. S.D. Tex. 2005)**

Because the court determined that the debtors were ineligible, and thus no case was commenced, the court found that the appropriate remedy for their ineligibility was to strike their petitions rather than dismiss their cases.

III.D *Wyttenbach v. C.I.R.,* **382 B.R. 726 (S.D. Tex. 2008)**

Striking the petition and retroactively annulling the automatic stay is a permissible remedy for an individual's noncompliance with the credit counseling requirement.

III.D.1 *Adams v. Finlay,* **2006 WL 3240522 (S.D.N.Y. Nov. 3, 2006)**

The bankruptcy judge acted within her judicial power when striking a petition where the debtor failed to obtain credit counseling prior to filing. "Failure to receive counseling in compliance with the statute is not jurisdictional, rather it goes to whether the petition states a claim upon which relief can be granted." Therefore, striking the petition rather than dismissal was a proper remedy.

III.D.1   *In re Elmendorf,* 345 B.R. 486 (Bankr. S.D.N.Y. 2006)

Court concluded that dismissal for cause pursuant to 11 U.S.C. §707(a) is not always the appropriate disposition of a petition that has been filed by a debtor ineligible for bankruptcy relief pursuant to 11 U.S.C. §109(h), and that the "court may choose to strike or dismiss a petition in view of the particular circumstances sub juidice in the exercise of its equitable powers pursuant to §105(a) to carry out Congressional intent that individuals receive credit counseling before filing for bankruptcy relief."

III.D.1   *In re Rios,* 336 B.R. 177 (Bankr. S.D.N.Y. 2005)

Putative debtor, who neither sought prepetition credit counseling nor made the appropriate certification to the court evidencing eligibility for an exemption from the credit counseling requirement, never properly commenced a case and, thus, the petition would be stricken, as opposed to dismissed.

III.D.1   *In re Thompson,* 344 B.R. 899 (Bankr. S.D. Ind. 2006), *vacated as moot,* 249 Fed. Appx. 475 (7th Cir. 2007)

When a putative debtor who files a bankruptcy petition is ineligible because he or she did not comply with BAPCPA's credit counseling requirements, the proper remedy is to strike the petition, not to dismiss the case, and the filing of a petition by an ineligible debtor triggers the automatic stay, even though no "case" has been commenced.

III.D.2   *In re Cannon,* 376 B.R. 847 (Bankr. M.D. Tenn. 2006)

Dismissal of chapter 13 case, as opposed to striking of the bankruptcy petition, was the appropriate outcome where individuals were ineligible to be debtors due to their failure to have obtained the requisite prepetition credit counseling.

III.D.2 *In re Dillard,* **2006 WL 3658485 (Bankr. M.D. Ga. Dec. 11, 2006)**

The appropriate method for dealing with the case of an ineligible debtor is the dismissal of the case because "the eligibility question is not jurisdictional and does not prevent an ineligible debtor from commencing a case and having that case dismissed."

III.D.2 *In re Dyer,* **381 B.R. 200 (Bankr. W.D.N.C. 2007)**

Petition filed by debtor who, due to lack of prepetition credit counseling, is not eligible to be bankruptcy debtor, is not legal nullity which has to be stricken, but rather is subject to being dismissed.

III.D.2 *In re Enloe,* **373 B.R. 123 (Bankr. D. Colo. 2007)**

Mere fact that debtors, as result of their attorney's error, did not file for chapter 7 relief until 189 days after they received credit counseling did not warrant dismissal of case. "Credit counseling" requirement imposed as prerequisite to individual's being eligible for bankruptcy relief is not jurisdictional, and until bankruptcy court determines debtor's eligibility, bankruptcy case actually exists, which cannot thereafter be deemed a nullity simply by striking the case.

III.D.2 *In re Falcone,* **370 B.R. 462 (Bankr. D. Mass. 2007)**

Appropriate remedy, upon finding that debtor had filed for chapter 13 relief without satisfying credit counseling requirement and without establishing requisite grounds for temporary waiver or exemption from credit counseling was order dismissing, rather than striking as void *ab initio*, the debtor's chapter 13 case.

III.D.2 *In re Mason,* **2007 WL 433077 (E.D. Ky. Feb. 5, 2007)**

District court overturned the bankruptcy court's decision to strike the petition rather than dismiss the case. The district court found that the bankruptcy court had exceeded its jurisdiction under §105. The district court found that "there is no support for the remedy of striking a debtor's petition in the Bankruptcy Code. On the other hand, the dismissal remedy is explicitly set forth in section 707 and is not limited to the conditions enumerated in that section."

III.D.2   ***In re Swiatkowski*, 356 B.R. 581 (Bankr. E.D.N.Y. 2006)**

"The law is clear that, with limited exceptions, a Debtor must obtain credit counseling prior to filing in order to be eligible to file a petition in bankruptcy." Additionally, "the Court declines to follow that line of cases which 'strike' rather than dismiss petitions."

III.D.2   ***In re Tomco*, 339 B.R. 145 (Bankr. W.D. Pa. 2006)**

"Cause" for dismissal of a bankruptcy case is not limited to the enumerated statutory list(s). Debtor's ineligibility for bankruptcy relief constitutes one "cause" for dismissal of the case.   Further, she was ineligible to be a debtor. The proper remedy was for the bankruptcy court to dismiss the case, as opposed to striking the petition as void *ab initio*.

III.D.2   ***In re Wallace*, 338 B.R. 339 (Bankr. E.D. Ark. 2006)**

Chapter 13 debtor's failure to seek or obtain credit counseling prior to filing her bankruptcy petition, and failure to provide any certificate of exigent circumstances, rendered her ineligible for bankruptcy relief and necessitated dismissal of petition.

III.D.2   ***In re Wilson*, 346 B.R. 59 (Bankr. N.D.N.Y. 2006)**

Appropriate disposition, upon determination by bankruptcy court that debtors had not satisfied prepetition credit counseling requirement and were not entitled to extension based on exigent circumstances, was to dismiss, not strike, bankruptcy case.

III.E.1   ***In re Hubbard*, 332 B.R 285 (Bankr. S.D. Tex. 2005)**

Section 109(h)(2) excuses debtors from the credit counseling requirement where the U.S. Trustee determines that approved agencies are not reasonably able to provide such services in the given district. However, the debtor could not seek relief under this provision because the Southern District of Texas was not so classified.

III.E.1 ***In re McBride*, 354 B.R. 95 (Bankr. D. S.C. 2006)**

"The United States Trustees for Regions 4 and 21, respectively, have not determined that the approved credit counseling providers for South Carolina and the federal judicial districts of Georgia are not reasonably able to provide adequate services to debtors. Section 109(h)(2) does not afford the debtor an exemption."

III.E.1 ***In re Mingueta*, 338 B.R. 833 (Bankr. C.D. Cal. 2006)**

The U.S. Trustee has not found that there are insufficient accredited credit counselors in the Central District of California. Thus, credit counseling cannot be waived pursuant to §109(h)(2).

III.E.2.a.i ***In re Cobb*, 343 B.R. 204 (Bankr. E.D. Ark. 2006)**

The certification that a debtor must submit in order to obtain a temporary waiver of the credit counseling requirement must contain facts that are sworn to under oath. Here, the typed statement submitted by the *pro se* chapter 13 debtors, which was not sworn to under penalty of perjury, did not constitute a certification as required for debtors to obtain a temporary waiver of the credit counseling requirement, even though the document was signed by each and dated.

III.E.2.a.i ***In re DiPinto*, 336 B.R. 693 (Bankr. E.D. Pa. 2006)**

The court held that a statement signed by counsel was insufficient to meet the certification requirement; a token effort at obtaining credit counseling at 5:00 on the eve of the filing was insufficient, and imminent foreclosure on the day of the filing was not exigent where putative debtor did not sufficiently explain why he delayed in seeking assistance. Thus, the court dismissed the case.

III.E.2.a.i *In re Hubbard,* **332 B.R 285 (Bankr. S.D. Tex. 2005)**

An extension cannot be granted under the plain meaning of §109(h)(3) without an "affidavit, declaration or other certification as to its accuracy." A simple unverified motion would not suffice.

III.E.2.a.i *In re Hubbard,* **333 B.R. 373 (Bankr. S.D. Tex. 2005)**

Applications for consideration of exigent circumstances under §109(h)(3) are not sufficient to meet the requirements for a "certificate." Until such certifications were filed, the court refused to consider the exigency of the circumstances.

III.E.2.a.i *In re Hubbard,* **333 B.R. 377 (Bankr. S.D. Tex. 2005)**

Where debtors did not file an appropriate verified statement of exigent circumstances pursuant to §109(h)(3), but did later file a verified statement that they received the counseling post-petition, the debtors were still ineligible to be debtors on their petition date. Further, the court went on to restate its previous finding in the matter that applications and unsworn statements did not meet the requirements for this provision.

III.E.2.a.i *In re LaPorta,* **332 B.R. 879 (Bankr. D. Minn. 2005)**

Debtor's unsworn statements that she did an Internet search and could not find an accredited agency that she could afford to reach for such services, particularly where she did not make any attempts to actually contact such services, were insufficient to meet the criteria for exigent circumstances under §109(h)(3)

III.E.2.a.i *In re Mingueta,* **338 B.R. 833 (Bankr. C.D. Cal. 2006)**

To obtain a waiver of the prepetition credit counseling requirement, a putative debtor must meet all the requirements of §109(h)(3). An unsubstantiated request that does not specify the circumstances or the steps taken to attempt to obtain such counseling is insufficient.

III.E.2.a.i *In re Rodriguez*, 336 B.R. 462 (Bankr. D. Idaho 2005)

Debtor sought exemption from credit counseling requirement. The court determined that the certification must be a document in which debtors personally verify, in a form consistent with federal statute governing declarations, verifications and certificates submitted under penalty of perjury, the facts which they wish court to consider; exigent circumstances that are alleged must distinguish the debtor from those generally expected to comply with the requirement.

III.E.2.a.i *In re Wilson*, 346 B.R. 59 (Bankr. N.D.N.Y. 2006)

The bankruptcy court held that: (1) to obtain extension based on exigent circumstances of time to obtain credit counseling, debtors must have requested such counseling prepetition; (2) certification of exigent circumstances must be the certification of debtors, not their counsel; and (3) appropriate disposition, upon determination by bankruptcy court that debtors had not satisfied prepetition credit counseling requirement and were not entitled to extension based on exigent circumstances, was to dismiss, not strike, bankruptcy case. Both the term "waiver" and "exemption" are misnomers, since what the statute seeks to provide the debtor with is an "extension" of time to comply with the credit counseling requirements.

III.E.2.a.ii *In re Henderson*, 339 B.R. 34 (Bankr. E.D.N.Y. 2006)

While finding that the certification seeking a temporary exemption from the credit counseling requirement need not be signed under penalty of perjury, the court nonetheless found that the debtor's statement was insufficient where it did not distinguish her from other debtors expected to meet the credit counseling requirement.

III.E.2.a.ii *In re Talib*, 335 B.R. 417 (Bankr. W.D. Mo. 2005)

While the court found the debtor's unsworn statement to be sufficient under the provisions of §109(h)(3), the court found that the other conditions of the provision were not met where the debtor failed to request credit counseling prior to filing her petition. Thus, the case was dismissed due to lack of eligibility.

III.E.2.b.i *Clippard v. Bass*, 365 B.R. 131 (W.D. Tenn. 2007)

Request filed by *pro se* chapter 7 debtor for temporary deferral of "credit counseling" requirement that she had to satisfy as prerequisite to establishing her eligibility for bankruptcy relief could not be granted on "exigent circumstances" theory, where debtor, while certifying that credit counseling was offered in that district only once per month, and that next session would occur more than one week later, did not explain why she had to file her petition immediately, and why she could not have waited until after attending this monthly session in order to file her petition, and where debtor, in failing to specify when she had first requested credit counseling, did not provide sufficient information to permit court to determine that counseling could not have been obtained within five days of debtor's request.

III.E.2.b.i *In re Afolabi*, 343 B.R. 195 (Bankr. S.D. Ind. 2006)

Proper focus under the exigent circumstances extention for the prepetition credit counseling requirement is not on the circumstances that hastened or precipitated the bankruptcy filing, but on whether those circumstances or any other prevented the debtor from being able to obtain credit counseling prior to filing for bankruptcy. "As several other courts have pointed out, §109(h)'s requirements may lead to harsh and arguably inequitable results. However, enforcement of §109(h) is mandatory. The Court has no discretion but to dismiss a case when the debtor fails to file a certification in compliance with its provisions."

III.E.2.b.i *In re Anderson*, 2006 WL 314539 (Bankr. N.D. Iowa Feb. 6, 2006)

Failure to show facts and circumstances surrounding garnishment of wages and timing of payment of such wages was insufficient to show exigency. Without specifying when wages are to be paid and why a filing was necessary before the counseling could be obtained, there was no showing of exigency. Further, where co-debtor did not sign statement regarding exigency, his case was dismissed outright.

III.E.2.b.i *In re Carey*, 341 B.R. 798 (Bankr. M.D. Fla. 2006)

The debtors did not meet the requirements of §109(h) where they failed to contact the credit counseling agency until half an hour after they filed their petition and did not receive the counseling until after the petition.

III.E.2.b.i *In re Carr*, 344 B.R. 774 (Bankr. N.D. W.Va. 2006)

Chapter 13 debtor was not entitled to temporary waiver, based on exigent circumstances, of credit counseling requirement imposed by BAPCPA, even assuming he could show exigent circumstances based on impending mortgage foreclosure sale, where debtor did not request credit counseling services from an approved nonprofit budget and credit counseling agency before filing his petition, and thus could not show that he had requested, but been unable to obtain such services.

III.E.2.b.i *In re Childs*, 335 B.R. 623 (Bankr. D. Md. 2005)

In consolidated cases, the consensus of the bankruptcy court judges was that: (1) debtors demonstrated "exigent circumstances" by asserting the imminent sale of their property at foreclosure and/or their imminent eviction from their residences; (2) debtors' certification of postpetition credit counseling was insufficient to grant a waiver of credit counseling; (3) certifications that did not mention any attempt by debtors to obtain credit counseling or that stated that debtors were unable to obtain credit counseling were insufficient to grant a waiver of credit counseling; and (4) debtors' failure to file satisfactory certifications of waiver of credit counseling and/or proper certificates of credit counseling required dismissal of their cases.

III.E.2.b.i *In re Davenport*, **335 B.R. 218 (Bankr. M.D. Fla. 2005)**

While the court found that the debtor had shown exigent circumstances, relief from the requirements of §109(h) was not available because she failed to request credit counseling before filing. The fact that the debtor received such counseling postpetition did not cure the error. Since the debtor was ineligible to be a debtor, the case was dismissed.

III.E.2.b.i *In re DiPinto*, **336 B.R. 693 (Bankr. E.D. Pa. 2006)**

The court held that a statement signed by counsel was insufficient to meet the certification requirement; a token effort at obtaining credit counseling at 5:00 on the eve of the filing was insufficient, and imminent foreclosure on the day of the filing was not exigent where putative debtor did not sufficiently explain why he delayed in seeking assistance. Thus, the court dismissed the case.

III.E.2.b.i *In re Dixon*, **338 B.R. 383 (B.A.P. 8th Cir. 2006)**

A bankruptcy court's decision that the threatened loss of a chapter 13 debtor's home at a foreclosure sale scheduled to occur one day after the bankruptcy petition was filed did not rise to the level of exigent circumstances which merited a waiver of the prepetition credit counseling requirement of BAPCPA was not an abuse of discretion. The debtor had ample advance notice of the foreclosure sale, but waited until one day prior thereto to contact an attorney. The requirement that the debtor, to receive a temporary waiver of the credit counseling requirement of BAPCPA, must demonstrate exigent circumstances meriting such a waiver, has at least two substantive components: first, there must be exigent circumstances; and, second, those circumstances must merit a waiver.

III.E.2.b.i *In re Gee*, **332 B.R. 602 (Bankr. W.D. Mo. 2005)**

"The Debtor can be eligible for a waiver under §109(h) (3) only if each of the following three requirements is met:

(1) the certification describes exigent circumstances that merit a waiver; (2) it states that the debtor requested credit counseling services from an approved agency, but was unable to obtain the services during the five-day period beginning on the date on which the debtor made the request; and (3) the certification is satisfactory to the Court. These requirements are stated in the conjunctive, meaning that each of the three requirements must be met."

III.E.2.b.i *In re Hedquist*, 342 B.R. 295 (B.A.P. 8th Cir. 2006)

Bankruptcy court's decision that debtors' delay in waiting to file bankruptcy petition until eve of mortgage foreclosure sale, despite fact that debtors had ample notice thereof, did not constitute "exigent circumstance," such as might permit temporary waiver of prepetition credit counseling requirement, was not abuse of discretion.

III.E.2.b.i *In re Henderson*, 339 B.R. 34 (Bankr. E.D.N.Y. 2006)

While finding that the certification seeking a temporary exemption from the credit counseling requirement need not be signed under penalty of perjury, the court nonetheless found that the debtor's statement was insufficient where it did not distinguish her from other debtors expected to meet the credit counseling requirement.

III.E.2.b.i *In re Hoshan*, 2008 WL 81994 (E.D. Pa. Jan. 7, 2008)

"The credit counseling requirement is not jurisdictional... The appellant did not get credit counseling until after she had filed her petition, and she did not seek an exigent circumstances waiver. Her family situation, while difficult, does not rise to the level of those cases in which courts avoid manifest injustice by waiving the credit counseling requirements."

III.E.2.b.i *In re LaPorta*, 332 B.R. 879 (Bankr. D. Minn. 2005)

Debtor's unsworn statements that she did an internet search and could not find an accredited agency which she could afford to reach for such services, particularly where she did not make any attempts to actually contact such services, were insufficient to meet the criteria for exigent circumstances under §109(h)(3).

III.E.2.b.i *In re Latovljevic,* 343 B.R. 817 (Bankr. N.D. W.Va. 2006)

Chapter 13 debtor who, though incarcerated at federal correctional institution, was not incapacitated or disabled in any way, and who made no attempt to avail himself of opportunities available to him to obtain credit counseling prepetition by telephone, was not entitled to temporary waiver or exemption from credit counseling requirement, so that his chapter 13 case had to be dismissed on ground that he was not eligible for such relief.

III.E.2.b.i *In re Piontek,* 346 B.R. 126 (Bankr. W.D. Pa. 2006)

The bankruptcy court held that: (1) debtor who lacks sufficient resources to pay for credit counseling may, under the right circumstances, have *de facto* "inability" to obtain pre-bankruptcy credit counseling, and this "inability" to pay for credit counseling may be a "satisfactory" reason for court to grant temporary waiver of the credit counseling requirement; but (2) debtors' alleged lack of financial resources to pay, prepetition, the two $50.00 fees that allegedly would have been required for both debtors to obtain prepetition credit counseling was not sufficiently established by evidence in record.

III.E.2.b.i *In re Postlethwait,* 353 B.R. 428 (Bankr. W.D. Pa. 2006)

Certification of exigent circumstances filed by chapter 13 debtor requesting a temporary waiver of the credit counseling requirement, in reciting only that the debtor had contacted two agencies in an unsuccessful attempt to obtain the required counseling roughly 40 minutes before her petition was filed, and six days prior to the creditor's sale that was alleged to be the exigent circumstance that necessitated the prompt filing of petition, did not sufficiently allege "inability" on debtor's part to obtain the required counseling.

III.E.2.b.i *In re Randolph*, **342 B.R. 633 (Bankr. M.D. Fla. 2005)**

The "exigent circumstances" exception to the credit counseling requirement does not extend to a debtor who "simply fails to prioritize the counseling requirement."

III.E.2.b.i *In re Rendler*, **368 B.R. 1 (Bankr. D. Minn. 2007)**

Case had to be dismissed on eligibility grounds, given that debtor-inmate had not requested temporary waiver of credit counseling requirement based on exigent circumstances, and would not have benefited therefrom in any event given his ongoing inability to obtain such counseling, and given that debtor's inability to obtain counseling was not result of incapacity, disability or service in military combat zone, as those terms were narrowly defined in Code provision permitting, in very limited circumstances, a permanent waiver of credit counseling requirement.

III.E.2.b.i *In re Rodriguez*, **336 B.R. 462 (Bankr. D. Idaho 2005)**

Debtor sought exemption from credit counseling requirement. The court determined that the certification must be document in which debtors personally verify, in form consistent with federal statute governing declarations, verifications and certificates submitted under penalty of perjury, the facts which they wish the court to consider; exigent circumstances that are alleged must distinguish the debtor from those generally expected to comply with the requirement.

III.E.2.b.i *In re Shea*, **2008 WL 80245**
(Bankr. E.D. Va. Jan. 7, 2008)

"Absent a request for services and the agency's inability to provide counseling within the five-day period, the court has no power to grant a request for waiver, no matter how compelling the circumstances."

III.E.2.b.i *In re Talib*, 335 B.R. 417 (Bankr. W.D. Mo. 2005)

While the court found the debtor's unsworn statement to be sufficient under the provisions of §109(h)(3), the court found that the other conditions of the provision were not met where the debtor failed to request credit counseling prior to filing her petition. Thus, the case was dismissed due to lack of eligibility.

III.E.2.b.i *In re Talib*, 335 B.R. 424 (Bankr. W.D. Mo. 2005)

On a motion for a rehearing of the dismissal of the debtor's case, the court determined that while requiring prospective debtor's to certify that credit counseling could not have been obtained within five days in order to obtain a temporary waiver may result in harsh rulings, such requirement did not rise to the level of absurdity so as to allow the bankruptcy court to interpret the statute other than via its plain meaning.

III.E.2.b.i *In re Toccaline*, 2006 WL 2081517 (Bankr. D. Conn. 2006)

The court found that while impending foreclosure in the wake of failed attempts at refinancing was an "exigent circumstance" and met the requirements of §109(h)(1), the inability to get counseling due to inability to pay the $50 fee within the five-day period was not sufficient to meet the requirements of §109(h)(3)(A)(ii). Thus, the court dismissed the petitioner's case.

III.E.2.b.i *In re Tomco*, 339 B.R. 145 (Bankr. W.D. Pa. 2006)

Where individual seeking chapter 13 relief acknowledged that she contacted no approved credit counseling agency before she filed her bankruptcy petition, so that her certificate of exigent circumstances was deficient and she was ineligible to be a debtor, the proper remedy was for the bankruptcy court to dismiss the case, as opposed to striking the petition as void *ab initio*.

III.E.2.b.i *In re Valdez,* **335 B.R. 801 (Bankr. S.D. Fla. 2005)**

Ignorance of the requirement for credit counseling until a time in which it was too late to obtain such counseling was not sufficient to be an exigent circumstance pursuant to §109(h)(3).

III.E.2.b.i *In re Wilson,* **346 B.R. 59 (Bankr. N.D.N.Y. 2006)**

The bankruptcy court held that: (1) to obtain extension, based on exigent circumstances, of time to obtain credit counseling, debtors must have requested such counseling prepetition; (2) certification of exigent circumstances must be the certification of debtors, not their counsel; and (3) appropriate disposition, upon determination by bankruptcy court that debtors had not satisfied prepetition credit counseling requirement and were not entitled to extension based on exigent circumstances, was to dismiss, not strike, bankruptcy case.   Both the term "waiver" and "exemption" are misnomers, since what the statute seeks to provide the debtor with is an "extension" of time to comply with the credit counseling requirements.

III.E.2.b.ii *In re Giambrone,* **365 B.R. 386 (Bankr. W.D.N.Y. 2007)**

Where chapter 13 debtors requested credit counseling services on the day prior to their bankruptcy filing, which also was the day prior to the scheduled foreclosure sale of their real property, were unable to obtain those services before bankruptcy, and ultimately completed credit counseling on the fifth day after their request, the bankruptcy court could grant an extension of time to complete credit counseling, even though credit counseling was available within five days, but not before the exigent event; when exigent circumstances require bankruptcy protection in fewer than five days, the window for completion of counseling must collapse into the amount of time that is available, and the test is not whether the agency can provide a counseling session within five days, but whether in the context of their circumstances, the debtors can complete within five days the counseling that must otherwise occur prior to that exigent moment when a bankruptcy filing is necessary.

III.E.2.b.ii *In re Henderson* 364 B.R. 906 (Bankr. N.D. Tex. 2007)

Foreclosure on a family home is a circumstance requiring immediate aid or action, particularly where the state in question has nonjudicial foreclosure. Further, the statute was ambiguous such that the statute could be interpreted to apply to the debtor who requested counseling services but was not able to obtain those services through duration of the five-day period beginning on the date which the request was made or to the debtor who requested services but was unable to obtain them at a point during the course or in the five-day period beginning on the date on which requested was made.

III.E.2.b.ii *In re Romero*, 349 B.R. 616 (Bankr. N.D. Cal. 2006)

Would-be chapter 7 debtors who, three days before filing for bankruptcy relief, had requested credit counseling from approved agency but been unable to obtain it within requisite five-day period specified by statute, and who had need to file for bankruptcy in order to prevent garnishment of debtor-husband's wages, sufficiently established requisite "exigent circumstances" and were entitled to temporary waiver of credit counseling requirement.

III.E.2.b.ii *In re Star*, 341 B.R. 830 (Bankr. E.D. Va. 2006)

The court found that the debtor's incarceration was not the sort of incapacitation or disability that would exempt the debtor from credit counseling pursuant to §109(h)(4). However, the court did find that the incarceration was sufficient to meet the exigent circumstances temporary exemption.

III.E.3.a.i *In re Latovljevic*, 343 B.R. 817 (Bankr. N.D. W.Va. 2006)

Chapter 13 debtor who, though incarcerated at federal correctional institution, was not incapacitated or disabled in any way, and who made no attempt to avail himself of opportunities available to him to obtain credit counseling prepetition by telephone, was not entitled to temporary waiver or exemption from credit counseling requirement, so that his chapter 13 case had to be dismissed on ground that he was not eligible for such relief.

III.E.3.a.i *In re McBride*, 354 B.R. 95 (Bankr. D. S.C. 2006)

Debtor's incarceration did not render him exempt from the credit counseling requirement as incapacitated or disabled. Thus, failure to obtain credit counseling was "cause" to dismiss the case.

III.E.3.a.i *In re Rendler*, 368 B.R. 1 (Bankr. D. Minn. 2007)

Case had to be dismissed on eligibility grounds, given that debtor-inmate had not requested temporary waiver of credit counseling requirement based on exigent circumstances and would not have benefited therefrom in any event given his ongoing inability to obtain such counseling, and given that debtor's inability to obtain counseling was not result of incapacity, disability or service in military combat zone, as those terms were narrowly defined in Code provision permitting, in very limited circumstances, a permanent waiver of credit counseling requirement.

III.E.3.a.i *In re Star*, 341 B.R. 830 (Bankr. E.D. Va. 2006)

The court found that the debtor's incarceration was not the sort of incapacitation or disability that would exempt the debtor from credit counseling pursuant to §109(h)(4). However, the court did find that the incarceration was sufficient to meet the exigent circumstances temporary exemption.

III.E.3.a.ii *In re Gates*, 2007 WL 4365474 (Bankr. E.D. Cal. Dec. 12, 2007)

"The [incarcerated] debtor is 'disabled' within the meaning ascribed in Section 109(h)(4)… He is therefore unable to physically attend a personal financial management course.

He also lacks access to the Internet and due to constraints placed by the California Department of Corrections, debtor cannot contact debtor education agencies by phone."

III.E.3.a.ii *In re Vollmer,* **361 B.R. 811 (Bankr. E.D. Va. 2007)**

Incarcerated chapter 7 debtor, who had no telephone or computer access other than ability to make collect calls, was unable to participate in required credit counseling and financial management courses, and therefore permanent waiver of those requirements was warranted, even though debtor's imprisonment, standing alone, was not "disability" sufficient to merit waiver of counseling requirement.

III.F   *In re Lilliefors,* **379 B.R. 608 (Bankr. E.D. Va. 2007)**

"The debtor is judicially estopped from benefiting by obtaining dismissal of his case for non-compliance with §109(h)(1). The debtor's certification under penalty of perjury that he completed credit counseling within 180 days before filing his bankruptcy petition, a requirement to commence his case, is adequate, unless challenged, to satisfy the credit counseling requirement. He may not now disavow that statement because creditors will be prejudiced if the case is dismissed...Because the debtor is judicially estopped from denying that he completed the requisite credit counseling, it is not necessary that a credit counseling certificate be filed."

III.F   *In re Mendez,* **367 B.R. 109 (B.A.P. 9th Cir. 2007)**

In the case at bar, debtor waived strict compliance with the pre-bankruptcy credit counseling requirements, and so was not entitled to use her noncompliance offensively, as a basis for dismissal; the bankruptcy court did not abuse its discretion in denying the motion to dismiss based on debtor's contentions that her bankruptcy papers were forged, that she did not intend to file a bankruptcy case, and that she did not want to be in bankruptcy.

III.F   *In re Parker*, 351 B.R. 790 (Bankr. N.D. Ga. 2006)

(1) debtor who, after becoming aware that entity from which he obtained credit counseling prepetition was not an approved credit counseling agency, had not immediately moved to dismiss case, but requested extension of time to obtain credit counseling from approved agency postpetition, waived right to rely on ineligibility provision as basis for voluntarily dismissing case; (2) debtor was judicially estopped from belatedly moving to voluntarily dismiss case; and (3) "automatic dismissal" language in bankruptcy statute providing that a case shall be automatically dismissed if debtor fails to file payment advices or other required information within 45 days of petition date did not mean that chapter 7 debtor, after becoming dissatisfied with progress of case when trustee moved to sell the principal asset that debtor sought to retain, could obtain determination that case had been dismissed based on his failure to file payment advices.

III.F   *In re Racette*, 343 B.R. 200 (Bankr. E.D. Wis. 2006)

Prior chapter 13 case filed by debtors who, contrary to representation made on face of prior petition, had not received prepetition credit counseling and were not eligible to be bankruptcy debtors was not mere nullity that bankruptcy court could strike and not treat as prior case for purpose of deciding what type of stay arose in second chapter 13 case which debtors filed the same date that prior case was dismissed; prior case, which was administered for almost 90 days, and in which trustee was appointed, meeting of creditors was held, order was entered requiring debtors to begin making plan payments, and motion for relief from stay was filed, was treated as case and not as mere nullity by all parties in interest.

III.F   *In re Timmerman*, 379 B.R. 838
             (Bankr. N.D. Iowa 2007)

Bankruptcy court would exercise its discretion not to dismiss, on debtors' own motion, bankruptcy case which they had originally commenced as case under chapter 12, before it was converted to chapter 7, though debtors had not satisfied prepetition credit counseling requirement and were ineligible for bankruptcy relief, where debtors had proceeded in bankruptcy and enjoyed its benefits for roughly 21 months and sought to voluntarily dismiss their case only after objections were filed to debtors' homestead exemption, and after proceeding was commenced to deny debtors a discharge.

III.F *In re Warren*, 378 B.R. 640 (N.D. Cal. 2007)

The bankruptcy court did not err in its determination judicial estoppel could act to prevent the debtor from dismissing his own case for failure to obtain the required credit counseling.

III.G *In re Hassett*, 341 B.R. 832 (Bankr. E.D. Va. 2006)

In light of newness of provision of BAPCPA that debtor violated by failing to file certification that she had completed course in personal financial management within 45 days of first date set for meeting of creditors, bankruptcy court would reopen her chapter 7 case, which was closed without granting debtor a discharge, to give debtor an opportunity to file and properly notice the required motion to extend time to file certificate of financial management; if debtor prevailed on merits of such a motion, then she would receive her discharge.

III.G *In re Knight*, 349 B.R. 681 (Bankr. D. Idaho 2006)

Debtor's desire to file certificate of his completion of financial management course, as required for him to obtain discharge, constituted "cause" to reopen case. However, "appropriate circumstances" did not exist for waiver of filing fee that chapter 7 debtor would otherwise have been required to pay on grant of his motion to reopen bankruptcy case to allow him to file certificate of his completion of financial management course, as required under BAPCPA for debtor to obtain chapter 7 discharge, where debtor was represented by experienced counsel, who admitted to having received notices from court of need to file certificate and of consequences of failing to do so, but counsel had nonetheless failed to advise court of difficulties that debtor was encountering in obtaining the required certificate and never requested that case remain open to allow debtor to obtain and file necessary certificate.

III.G ***In re Lauro*, 2007 WL 4180683 (W.D. Pa. Nov. 20, 2007)**

In a case where the debtors were not advised by their counsel to file their post-petition financial management course certificate even though they completed the course within the time limit, the court held that "despite their failure to comply with the forty-five-day time limit specified by Interim Bankruptcy Rule 1007(c), the [Debtors] are entitled under Pioneer to an equitable inquiry regarding the issue raised with respect to excusable neglect…This court finds that the [Debtors] meet their burden of showing excusable neglect and holds as a matter of equity that their bankruptcy case will be reopened."

IV ***In re Beacher*, 358 B.R. 917 (Bankr. S.D. Tex. 2007)**

In consolidated cases, debtors were not required to file offical means test form where debts were not primarily consumer in nature, and dismissal of petition was not warranted on ground that debtors failed to file form.

IV ***In re Brown*, 376 B.R. 601 (Bankr. S.D. Tex. 2007)**

Under the means test, debtors could not deduct, as "applicable monthly expense amount" specified under the IRS's National and Local Standards, a vehicle ownership expense for motor vehicles which they owned outright, but disposable income available to debtors warranted dismissal of case based on totality of circumstances.

| IV | ***In re Cadwallder,*** **2007 WL 1864154 (Bankr. S.D. Tex. June 28, 2007)** |

U.S. Trustee's motion to dismiss determined to be timely and, thus, prosecutable. Debtor's objections to motion related to inadequacy of the U.S. Trustee's statement under Bankruptcy Code §704(b) overruled, and the objection to the timeliness of the U.S. Trustee's motion to dismiss was overruled.

| IV | ***In re Copeland,*** **2006 WL 2578877 (Bankr. S.D. Tex. Sept. 5, 2006)** |

The court concluded that individual chapter 7 debtors with primarily business debts are required to file form B22A.

| IV | ***In re Fox,*** **370 B.R. 639 (Bankr. D. N.J. 2007)** |

Court determined that the means test applied only to those cases commenced under chapter 7 and excluded cases converted from other chapters.

| IV | ***In re Hill,*** **328 B.R. 490 (Bankr. S.D. Tex. 2005)** |

In consolidated cases, court dismissed two cases on lack-of-need theory, as constituting a "substantial abuse" of provisions of chapter 7 where: (1) combined monthly income exceeded $13,600.00 and (2) debtors made more than $300 in monthly voluntary contributions to retirement plan.

| IV | ***In re Kellett,*** **379 B.R. 332 (Bankr. D. Or. 2007)** |

Debtors in cases converted to chapter 7 must file a form 22A, but court also concluded that this requirement could be waived in specific circumstances and so waived the requirement.

| IV | ***In re Kerr,*** **2007 WL 2119291 (Bankr. W.D. Wash. July 18, 2007)** |

The debtor was required, upon conversion of the case, to complete and file the bankruptcy form implementing the statutory test.

IV   *In re King,* 2008 WL 1808522
        (Bankr. S.D. Tex. Apr. 18, 2008)

        The presumption of abuse arose under the means test. The
        U.S. Trustee's motion for summary judgment granted and
        the case dismissed.

IV   *In re Leary,* 2008 WL 1782636
        (Bankr. S.D. Tex. Apr. 16, 2008)

        Debtors not allowed deduction for secured debts on
        surrendered property but allowed the deduction for vehicles
        as specified in the IRS's National and State Standards
        without reference to the IRS's Internal Revenue Manual.

IV   *In re Perfetto,* **361 B.R. 27 (Bankr. D. R.I. 2007)**

        The debtor was required, upon conversion of her case, to
        complete and file bankruptcy form implementing statutory
        means test.

IV   *In re Singletary,* **354 B.R. 455 (Bankr. S.D. Tex. 2006)**

        In applying the means test, the mere act of declaring an
        intent to surrender collateral on a statement of intention
        does not extinguish debtors' right to deduct those payments
        as being "scheduled as contractually due," but debtors may
        not deduct payments on collateral that already has been
        surrendered as of the motion date.

V   *In re Belcher,* **369 B.R. 465 (Bankr. E.D. Ark. 2007)**

        Debtors could not modify their confirmed chapter 13
        plan to provide that lender's perfected purchase money
        security interest in motor vehicle would be satisfied in full
        by payment of insurance proceeds and transfer of wrecked
        vehicle to it, even though wreck was unanticipated event,
        where debtors had elected to retain vehicle and to pay
        entire amount of lender's claim plus interest. 11 U.S.C.A.
        §1329.

V   *In re Demske*, 372 B.R. 85 (Bankr. M.D. Fla. 2007)

Lack of evidence as to how mortgage refinancing affected debtors' disposable income, either positively or negatively, prevented court from granting debtors' motion to modify plan to pay off their creditors early with proceeds of mortgage refinancing.

V   *In re Disney*, 386 B.R. 292 (Bankr. D. Colo. 2008)

The court held that a creditor could be bound by the debtor's post-confirmation modification of a chapter 13 plan. Moreover, the court held that a chapter 13 debtor may recharacterize an allowed secured claim post-confirmation following foreclosure or surrender of collateral and treat the resulting deficiency claim in the modified plan. The court further found that cause existed to reconsider the allowance of the creditor's claim. Thus, the debtor could modify his treatment of the creditor's claim under his plan to provide for the claim to be paid as an unsecured claim. Finally, the reclassification of a creditor's claim and modification of its treatment under a confirmed plan did not violate the creditor's due process rights.

V   *In re Ireland*, 366 B.R. 27 (Bankr. W.D. Ark. 2007)

Debtors, who suffered substantial reduction in income after filing their bankruptcy petition, were not prohibited by BAPCPA from modifying their chapter 13 plan after confirmation to reduce payments to unsecured creditors, despite contention that their "current monthly income" used to calculate plan payments was permanently fixed at time they filed petition.

V   *In re Meza*, 467 F.3d 874 (5th Cir. 2006)

Sections 1329(a) and 1329(b)(2), when considered together, "show that, when a modification request is timely filed, the completion of the plan and eventual discharge of the debtor is stayed until the bankruptcy court is allowed to consider the modification on its merits. A contrary result would encourage gamesmanship on behalf of debtors and prevent them from repaying creditors 'to the extent of [their] capabilit[ies].' *In re Arnold*, 869 F.2d at 242 ('Certainly Congress did not intend for debtors who experience substantially improved financial conditions after confirmation to avoid paying more to their creditors.')"

V   ***In re Murphy*, 474 F.3d 143 (4th Cir. 2007)**

Refinancing a home mortgage was not a substantial change in the financial condition, as required to modify a chapter 13 plan. Moreover, the court held that a sale of the debtor's condominium was a "substantial and unanticipated change" in the debtor's financial circumstances and the proposed modification of the chapter 13 was warranted.

V   ***In re Nichols*, 440 F.3d 850 (6th Cir. 2006)**

Postconfirmation plan modification could be approved though it would likely cause creditor to become undersecured. A modified chapter 13 plan proposed by debtors to cure a postconfirmation default resulting from the debtor-husband's temporary loss of employment, under which the debtors proposed to use their disposable income first to cure a default in their mortgage payments and to delay any payment to a purchase-money motor vehicle lender for nearly one year, did not impair the lender's lien rights contrary to the Fifth Amendment, and bankruptcy court did not abuse its discretion in approving the modified plan. While this delay in payment would likely cause the lender to become slightly undersecured, the lender, as of the date of the hearing on the modified plan, was still protected by a slight equity cushion in vehicle. Moreover, the lender had already received a significant portion of the total amount due, having received plan payments alone of roughly $14,300 on the original $14,000 debt, and would receive most of what it bargained for at the start of the parties' relationship, including interest.

VI   ***In re Bauer*, 343 B.R. 234 (Bankr. W.D. Mo. 2006)**

Potential complications arising from the dual administration, after chapter 7 debtors' death, of their bankruptcy and probate estates did not warrant dismissal of bankruptcy cases or suspension of proceedings therein.

VI   ***In re Lucio*, 251 B.R. 705 (Bankr. W.D. Tex. 2000)**

(1) chapter 7 case can continue notwithstanding the death of debtor; (2) debtor's daughter could not appear at first meeting of creditors as substitute for deceased debtor; (3) personal representative of debtor's probate estate could appear on behalf of debtor at creditors' meeting; and (4) it might be necessary to continue first meeting of creditors to afford personal representative a fair opportunity to obtain necessary letters from probate court.

VI   ***In re Oliver*, 279 B.R. 69 (Bankr. W.D.N.Y. 2002)**

Failure of chapter 7 debtor to appear at first meeting of creditors due to his death prior to that meeting did not constitute *per se* basis for dismissal of case, where debtor was current in satisfying his obligations under Bankruptcy Code at time of his death and U.S. Trustee made no showing that debtor's inability to appear at meeting of creditors would have meaningful adverse impact on case administration; in order to obtain dismissal, U.S. Trustee would have to show that decedent's administrator was inadequate substitute for chapter 7 debtor.

VI   ***In re Peterson*, 897 F.2d 935 (8th Cir. 1990)**

(1) under North Dakota law, debtor's death eight months after filing bankruptcy petition did not constitute abandonment of homestead exemption or cause it to lapse and revert back to bankruptcy estate, and (2) at time debtor filed his bankruptcy petition, he was entitled to homestead exemption.

VI   ***In re Robles*, 2007 WL 4410395 (Bankr. W.D. Tex. Dec. 13, 2007)**

"A dead debtor is not getting into any more trouble-at least not in this world. And the probate estate is hardly in danger of profligacy either (though perhaps the estate's beneficiaries perhaps should be required to complete an instructional course in financial management as a precondition to their receiving their inheritance?)."

VI   ***In re Trembulak*, 362 B.R. 205 (Bankr. D. N.J. 2007)**

"[C]learly the Debtor herein cannot participate in an instructional course on personal financial management and obviously such a course will not aid the Debtor in avoiding future financial distress. It seems palpably obvious that if a financial management course would be meaningless for an 81 year old, hearing-impaired debtor, suffering from prostate cancer, then such a course would likewise offer even less benefit to a deceased debtor."

NOW
at the ABI BOOKSTORE

Bankruptcy-A Survival Guide for Lenders, Second Edition

This book was developed specifically to assist lenders in understanding the bankruptcy process in business and consumer cases, and their role in that process. This updated edition addresses the changes with the 2005 amendments to the bankruptcy law and covers substantive bankruptcy issues, procedures and strategies for lenders. It features practical advice in the form of "sidebars" geared toward the protection of lenders' interests during a bankruptcy case, and glossaries of both bankruptcy terms and bankruptcy cases, as well as a list of commonly asked questions. Written with the non-attorney in mind, the text cross-references relevant terms and cases in the glossaries for further information, and highlights special points throughout. Executives and managers in banking, as well as turnaround specialists, and lenders in particular, will find the *Guide* an indispensable resource. Softbound, 176 pages. Members: $30; Non-members: $50

ABI Preference Handbook, Second Edition

Second only to the experience of filing a claim in bankruptcy, preference exposure is the most common experience a creditor will encounter in bankruptcy. Updated to address the 2005 changes to the Bankruptcy Code, *ABI's Preference Handbook, Second Edition* by David B. Wheeler (Moore & Van Allen) provides a streamlined guide to the "ins" and "outs" of preference claims and preference liability, and is written to appeal to lawyers and nonlawyers alike. Softbound, 90 pages.

Members: $25; non-members: $45

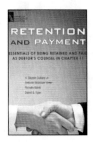

Retention and Payment: Essentials of Being Retained and Paid as Debtor's Counsel in Chapter 11

This book is a must-read for attorneys who may be generally unfamiliar with the chapter 11 process but who find themselves representing chapter 11 debtors. The handbook provides important practice pointers on obtaining court approval of the retention as debtor's bankruptcy counsel and obtaining court approval to be paid for services rendered to the debtor. It also contains samples of an engagement letter, a retention application and associated documents, and a fee application. Co-authored by H. Slayton Dabney Jr., the handbook provides an overview of the more significant issues chapter 11 counsel may encounter in navigating the retention and payment process. Softbound, 102 pages.

Members: $25; Non-members: $45

Browse these titles and our other publications at www.abiworld.org/abistore!

ABI Membership Application

Name _____

Firm/Company _____

Title/Profession _____

Address_____

City, State, Zip + 4 _____

Phone/Fax _____

E-mail Address _____

Annual Dues (please check one)

❏ General Membership   US $275

❏ Government/Academic (nonprofit)   US $95

❏ Student (full time)   US $20

Additional/Optional

❏ INSOL International   US $105

❏ ABI Endowment Contribution   US $45

Payable by Check or Credit Card

❏ Enclosed is my check payable to the American Bankruptcy Institute.

❏ Please charge to my credit card: ❏ Visa ❏ Amex ❏ MC

Account No._____

Exp. Date _____ Signature _____

Return to: American Bankruptcy Institute

44 Canal Center Plaza, Suite 400, Alexandria, VA 22314

Membership is on an individual basis and is valid one year from the enrollment date. Dues are not deductible as charitable contributions for tax purposes, but may be considered ordinary and necessary business expenses. Memberships are nontransferable.

Join ABI online at www.abiworld.org!